WHEN
IT'S
YOUR
TURN
TO
SPEAK

WHEN
IT'S
YOUR
TURN
TO
SPEAK

ORVIN LARSON Chairman of the Department of
Speech and Theatre, Brooklyn College, New York

 HARPER & BROTHERS
PUBLISHERS,
NEW YORK

To

HUGO A. CARLSON,

the best speech teacher I ever had

Grateful acknowledgment is made for permission to reprint material by the following authors:

Thomas H. Coulter, speech introducing Marguerite Higgins from *I Am Happy to Present*, compiled by Guy R. Lyle and Kevin Guinagh. Published by the H. W. Wilson Company, New York, 1953. Reprinted by permission of author.

Murray Banks, "How to Live With Yourself." Published by McCall's Magazine, New York, March, 1960. Reprinted by permission of publisher.

Henry J. Taylor, "Integrity: A Mighty Force," from *An American Speaks His Mind*. Published by Doubleday & Company, Inc., Garden City, 1957. Reprinted by permission of publisher.

Charles H. Brower, President, Batten, Barton, Durstine and Osborn, Inc., for excerpts from his speech, "The Year of the Rat," 1960.

FIRST EDITION

Library of Congress Catalog Card Number: 62-9911

CONTENTS

PREFACE

SPEAKING IN PUBLIC IS, MORE THAN EVER, A FIRST CONCERN of the executive, the professional man, the alert citizen. "Boom in Speechmaking," a recent feature in *Time* magazine, points out that "One of the biggest booms in the nation comes from all those businessmen who are getting up to speak." They aim not only to promote or sell their products but also to set forth their beliefs and goals.

"Society today demands from management a restatement of the purposes of free enterprise," says Clarence Randall, a former chairman of Inland Steel Company. "Our creed is being distorted by our enemies and we are not talking back. Sometimes I ask myself guiltily whether we are capable of talking back." As more men and women are realizing this lack, there is a great demand for practical speech courses, and speech bulks large in employee training.

I received a letter from the assistant to an executive who said that his chief was looking for private instruction in public speaking. Almost a paradox—*private* instruction in *public* speaking? Not really, for much learning takes place in private; this goes for speaking too.

This book is designed, therefore, as much for the reader who wants to study in private as for the student in a speech class.

The book aims to help not only people in business but men and women of all vocations, the officers and members of organizations and committees, and the individual in his role as a citizen. It is for all who would know how to prepare a good speech and how to put it across. It also deals with other situations that require skill in speaking: with committee and group discussion, including "brain-storming"; with conducting meetings and moderating programs; with the oral reading of data, reports, speeches, and television scripts. The book aims to equip you for any speech situation.

I have sought to compress into this book the experience of many years of teaching—to help you to gain poise, to help you to be effective in voice and bodily action, to aid you in pronunciation, to enable you to use language that is clear, graphic, and persuasive, to help you to think better.

The book aims at all times to be practical.

O. L.

Freeport, Long Island
February 1962

WHEN
IT'S
YOUR
TURN
TO
SPEAK

1   TODAY'S SPEAKER

Speak, and you sell, or unsell, yourself. speak and you make an image, to your credit or not. The image may not be the real you. It may be falsified by "nerves," by faults of voice or diction or bodily action, by shortcomings of logic or language. It may be falsified by a lack of know-how or of something to say or by an old habit of never saying anything. The adage, "Still waters run deep," has run into trouble with stagnant pools.

You may be interesting but your speech shows you dull. You may be bold but your speech shows you weak. You may be decisive but your speech contradicts you. You may be the answer to the quest for vice-presidents, but because of your speech you are always the "best man," never the groom. The number of muffed opportunities in the United States on a single day because of poor speech or non-speech is enough to unsettle a veteran statistician.

You may have heard of the demand in this country during recent years for English secretaries. One aspect of the demand is the desire of bosses for the English accent. In an article on the subject in the *New York Times Magazine,* May 1, 1960, Martha Weinman quotes the words of a junior executive: "That accent gets me, that's all. It gets everyone. Clients call, they're impressed. Friends call, they're impressed. Even my wife is impressed. It makes me feel like a big man." Though the accent may be an artificial, passing fancy of employers, the point is it is good speech that creates the favorable impression. It is not just accent. It is that plus poise, politeness, and a pleasant voice.

The highest judicial tribunal of the land, the United States Supreme Court, is not above appreciating the power of the spoken word. The men of that court like to hear arguments that are well delivered. Judicial and objective though the nine men are, they are interested in the *how* something is presented as well as in the *what*—interested indeed to the extent of being influenced by the *how*. Justice Harlan said of oral argument that it "may in many cases make the difference between winning and losing, no matter how good the briefs are."

Think of television, that gigantic and ever growing medium, which magnifies the defects of speakers as well as the virtues. Many among you will be, have been, or now are on television. How will you fare? There is an organization in New York City called *Executives On Camera* which provides training for men and women who are called upon to appear in corporation films or on closed circuit or regular television. The organization came into being because so many executives, as well as other people, have distracting mannerisms which the camera exaggerates. Some of the mannerisms are head bobbing, speaking from the side of the mouth, jiggling in a chair or swaying to and fro when standing, excessive gesturing, the frozen face or "dead-pan."

No one dares to say that the decisive factor in the outcome of the presidential campaign of 1960 was the speaking of the two candidates in their television debates. But the fact remains that a marked decline in Nixon's popularity set in after the first debate. His immediate post-convention margin over Kennedy, as indicated by polls, was substantial. Then came the first debate: It marred the public image of Richard Nixon; it enhanced that of John Kennedy. Nixon looked gaunt, grim, stiff, and ill at ease. Kennedy was natural, flexible, and buoyant. Moreover, and this was crucial, the "youth" and "inexperience" objections to Kennedy withered in the competence of his performance. As Jack Gould, television editor of the *New York Times* put it, after the second debate, October 6: "After two joint appearances it may be that TV more than anything else has disposed of the controversy over his youthfulness. The difference in the ages of the candidates now seems as small as it is." On November 3, Thursday preceding election day, James Reston, columnist of the *New York Times*, said that there was "general agreement" in Washington that Kennedy was going to win; he also said, "and nobody quite agrees on the reason." But in speculating about the "might-have-beens" of the campaign Reston asked: what "if Nixon had not given Kennedy the opportunity of the TV debates?" It is a fascinating question, to which I give this answer: the debates were the decisive factor in the campaign; Nixon would have won if it had not been for the debates. So get ready for your television appearances; they may come sooner than you think if they have not come already.

You can become an all-round good speaker. Good speakers are not born, they are made. Four elements go into their making: an efficient mind, an effective personality, know-how, and practice. This book tells you the *what* and *how* of good speaking. But you provide the practice.

Practice at the slightest opportunity, anywhere and any time. Impose upon the members of your family. Go to meetings of school boards, unions, business associations, service organizations, lodges, church committees, political groups—go to the meetings and speak whenever possible. Join a Toastmaster's Club; there are many in the country. Or organize a community group. In the days when the radio discussion program "Town Hall Tonight" was in its heyday, hundreds of Town Hall groups throughout the country would meet right after the program to continue the discussion. The members thus had weekly practice in this type of speaking. By looking around for opportunities for practice, you will unquestionably find them.

STAGE FRIGHT

You should know that stage fright puts you in the company of the great. One of the best talkers of the British Isles, on and off the platform, was George Bernard Shaw. It was not always so. Of his first public speech, before a debating society, The Zetetical Society, Shaw writes in *Sixteen Self Sketches*: "I started up and said something in the debate, and then, feeling that I had made a fool of myself, as in fact I had, I was so ashamed that I vowed I would join the society; go every week; speak in every debate; and become a speaker or perish in the attempt. I carried out this resolution. I suffered agonies that no one suspected."

Cornelia Otis Skinner, in common with almost all actors and actresses, suffers from first-night, and other night, jitters. She has often wondered why she didn't give up the gruesome business. She once asked her father, Otis, one of the immortals of the American stage, "how long one had to be in the theatre before outgrowing stage fright." He replied: "I have been in the theatre for fifty years and I've never outgrown it. Any actor who claims he is immune to stage fright is either lying or else he's no actor."

Stage fright is, in a sense, essential to an actor. The imagination and emotional sensitivity that cause stage fright also make the actor. The tensions of stage fright enable him to be expressive. If he were placid, his projection would be weak, his "presence" dull: he would be no actor.

For speakers, too, tension is essential. What if you were so calm before your hearers that you put them to sleep? Or so cool that they did not warm up? So count your nervousness not a liability but an asset to be turned into a capital gain. Control your nervousness, yes, and this is what practice will enable you to do. Practice and sense, or, if you please, a realistic view of yourself as a speaker and human being.

THREE HELPFUL ATTITUDES

First, don't take yourself so seriously. You are a human being with the faults, foibles, and virtues that flesh is heir to. Avoid perfectionism, a prime cause of stage fright. Perfectionism forces you to measure yourself against an impossible ideal of behavior. It stretches you to the breaking point. It unnerves you.

A second attitude is to realize that you have seen, heard, and felt things as no one else has. Though you may come from the same environment as others, your experience has been personally, uniquely, different.

A girl of eighteen held an audience spellbound as she talked of the care of bees. A saleslady spoke on types of customers, to the hilarity of her hearers. A worker in a factory specializing in abrasive papers made sandpaper appealing. A bank teller convinced his audience that ten dollar bills, one hundred dollar bills, one thousand dollar bills are as dull to him as potatoes to a grocery clerk. A youth from the slums of New York City alternately amused and chilled his hearers as he described, with visual aids and from personal experience, the weapons of gang "rumbles."

Whatever you are—farmer or nurse or auto mechanic, salesman or minister, lawyer or college student, secretary or housewife—wherever you have been or come from, whatever you have done, whatever in short has come into the ken of your senses and brain—even what emerges in dreams—all of this is grist for the speaker's mill. Do not discount it. One of the most successful lectures of all time was "Acres of Diamonds" by Russell Conwell. Its central theme was that opportunities are in our own backyard. You do not have to go to Timbuktu, you need not have scaled Mount Everest; you need not be a space man, an industrial tycoon, a movie star, or a United States Senator; take advantage of whatever you are and have now.

The third helpful attitude is of utmost importance to daily living as well as to improvement in speaking. It is the attitude of not being unduly concerned about tomorrow, of not worrying too much about a speech performance before it happens.

You should resolve right now to do what the Reverend E. Stanley Jones advises: "Live in day-tight compartments." This has two implications for speech development. First, it means that what you do today, in fact this very hour, is what will determine how well you will do next week or next month. If you are to make a speech next week, think today, this very hour, about your topic. Don't think about the impression you make next week; concentrate on your topic *now*. Let the future take care of itself. "Sufficient unto the day is the evil thereof." The second implication of the "day-tight compartment" is that progress is a matter of *small steps* forward.

I cannot urge too strongly upon you the practical importance, both in speech improvement and in daily living, of the "day-tight compartment."

> Life is hard
> By the yard
> But by the inch
> It's a cinch.

ABOUT FORGETTING AND A "SMALL" VOCABULARY

The best speakers forget with equanimity. But not being afraid to forget, they forget little. It is the novices who tremble at the prospect of forgetting a sentence, a phrase, a word. This fear of forgetting is one of the common causes of stage fright. It drives novices to write out a speech word for word and either read it instead of speak it or memorize it and deliver it like vocalizing robots. Or, worse still, they memorize it and then forget it. Herein lies a lesson: it is better to forget a point of an unmemorized speech than to forget all or most of a memorized one.

Forget about forgetting. Think about your topic, not about your future downfall. Work up an outline (more about outlines later). Go over the outline several times. Practice aloud from it. You will then remember your main points when you speak.

What if you do not remember everything. This may be all to the good. What you do not remember may not be remembered for the best of reasons, it was not worth remembering. Or something better occurs to you while you are speaking; this happens often to speakers whom a memorized speech does not freeze.

You may use notes while you speak. But do not make them so detailed that they amount to a verbatim speech. Detailed notes will keep your eyes on the notes, away from where they should be most of the time—on the audience.

Develop the extempore style of speaking. Be direct and conversational. Let most of the actual phrases and sentences that you use come to you while you speak. Too much advance formulation of ideas eliminates the spontaneity and sparkle of conversation.

"What you say about extemporizing a speech is all right for some but not for me. My trouble is a small vocabulary." Don't fool yourself. Your vocabulary is large enough. In a later chapter I shall have something to say about diversifying your speaking vocabulary, but now you have words aplenty to extemporize an idea—if you give yourself a chance. It is not that your vocabulary is small, it is that your fear, your imaginary fear, is large.

Novices think that they should mouth words in smoothly flowing, uninterrupted sequence. Novices are afraid of pause, they cannot stand silence. The seasoned speaker is not afraid to repeat himself or to begin a sentence over again; he is not afraid to pause and hunt a bit in his mind for the right word; he is not distressed by not getting the word instantly. This seems unnatural to the beginner and it scares him. One pause and he begins to sense disaster. Then he signals his distress to his audience. He may say, "Oh, pardon me," or "Oh, I just can't think of a word," or he indulges in the vocalized pause which is the "Ah, Ah, Ah, Ah" or "and-Ah, and-Ah" habit. One thing leads to another, to the discomfiture of both speaker and audience.

It is important to keep in mind just what an audience does *not* notice. It does not notice that you are about to collapse though you may think you are. It does not hear your pounding heart though you may think it does. It does not see that trembling leg. It does not feel that sweating palm.

So I say to you: "You're not one-tenth so bad as you think you are."

2 YOU FIND MATERIAL

HAVING SOMETHING TO SAY

"HOW LONG DID YOU WORK ON THAT SPEECH?" SOMEONE
asked Senator Daniel Webster about his famous "Reply to Hayne," delivered in the United States Senate on January 26 and 27, 1830.

"Twenty years," said Webster.

In this speech on the constitutional primacy of the Union—"Liberty
and union, now and forever, one and inseparable"—Webster rejected
the proposition of Senator Robert Hayne that the state which he repre-
sented, South Carolina, could nullify a federal law. Hayne had spoken
on January 21 and, the Senate adjourning, again on January 25.
Webster had little time to get ready but it was enough. His ideas had
developed over years of thoughtful devotion to the constitution and the
Union.

A good speech is not an overnight matter. You do not get a topic one
day and deliver a masterpiece the next. There is no such thing as an
inspiration of the moment. What seems to be an inspiration—not the
same as an impulse or a whim—is the final revelation of a process of
thought. Patrick Henry's "Give me liberty or give me death" speech
was the inspired expression of passionate conviction and thorough
preparation.

A good speech has to say something, which means that you must have
something to say. What does "something to say" mean? For one thing,
you believe in your ideas, you have convictions. For another, by experience, study, and thought, you acquire a body of knowledge on a subject,
that is, you acquire facts, lines of reasoning, vocabulary. What you say
may evoke dissent. If it also evokes the comment, "But I must admit he
makes a good case," or "Too bad that someone who knows so much can
be so wrong," then unmistakably you have something to say.

We have to rule out as a measure of "something to say" whether it is
accepted or not. The something may be that which makes sense to us
but not to others. Again, what impresses others as true may be to us
distortion or error.

Having something to say also means that you think clearly. You need not be a genius. In fact, genius can be a bar to clear thinking. Genius usually means a high degree of personal sureness, a sure source of errors in logic. See how renowned philosophers seldom, if ever, agree. Says no-nonsense Aristotle, "A is A," for example, that four-legged animal is a horse; says Hume, it is a horse only because I see it; says Kant, it is a horse because it agrees with my innate idea of horsiness; says Count Alfred Korzybski, the general semanticist, it is a unique horse of the moment of my perception (another moment, another horse). So we have here a horse *objective* (Aristotle), two horses *subjective* for opposite reasons (Hume and Kant), and one in a state of flux (Korzybski).

If one of the philosophers is right, the others are wrong. They cannot all be right; they can all be wrong. Either the thinking of three of them is off or the thinking of four of them is off.

It is a trained mind, rather than genius, that makes for clear thinking. A trained mind is the result of a mental regimen as much as a body in trim is the result of a physical regimen. A thinker can be trained, in the same way as a golf player, a dancer, or a surgeon is trained.

The trained mind works as follows:

1. It evaluates reasoning: disentangles fact and fancy, truth and prejudice, real reason and good reason.
2. It weighs data and source.
3. It searches for essentials, does not lose the forest for the trees.
4. It organizes what it takes in.
5. It expertly uses words.

The effective speaker has a trained mind. Effective speaking is effective thinking aloud.

This book is as much concerned with thinking as with speaking. Thus it deals with the essentials of a "liberal education." Note how the definition of a liberal education of the great English churchman and writer, Cardinal John Henry Newman, equals our concept of effective speaking: "the education which gives a man a clear, conscious view of his own opinions and judgments, a truth in developing them, an eloquence in expressing them, and a force in urging them. It teaches him to see things as they are, to get right to the point, to disentangle a skein of thought, to detect what is sophistical, and to discard what is irrelevant."

Do not think that a liberal education is something only for schools. A liberal education is a lifetime process. The crucial test of a liberal education is whether it continues when schooling is over.

If with the end of school one no longer, for instance, reads books, it is a good sign that an education did not "take." While the reading of books is no sure sign of an active mind, the non-reading of books is a sign of an inactive one. True, books are only one source of knowledge but they are indispensable to a speaker of parts. "Reading," writes Francis Bacon, "maketh a full man."

Where else do you get "something to say?" You should never overlook the riches in your own backyard. The metaphor applies even if you live in a tenth-floor apartment. First, explore your own vein; you may come upon a mother lode. Prod yourself with such questions as:

1. What am I really interested in?
2. What do I strongly believe in?
3. What are my pet peeves or big beefs?
4. What are my strong likes?
5. What have I done; where have I been; whom have I known?
6. What have I seen or heard today?

Such questions will uncover an amazing mine of attitudes, ideas, and facts. Do not ever think that you have nothing worth talking about; anyone who has enough interest in the arts of speech to read this book or any book on the subject has more than enough resources for stimulating speeches.

Suppose you have a speech to make and the topic is left up to you. The topic should come from your own interests but with concern, too, for the interests of your audience. In Chapter 5 audience interests will be given full treatment. Suppose among your concerns is your desire to give up smoking. You have tried several times to give it up. You suspect that it is harmful to you and you have read a good deal about cigarettes and lung cancer. You can assume that the problem of the habit will be of much interest to your audience, which, let us say, is an adult class in public speaking. You decide that since you are a specialist in breaking the habit you will speak on how to do it. You will not say much about the evils of smoking since you do not have the time or you feel that you are not qualified since the experts themselves disagree or you feel that your hearers are aware of the evils.

Now that you have chosen your topic, "How to Stop Smoking," what next? Take a sheet of paper and jot down whatever comes to you on the topic. Jot down everything. This is thinking. Thinking does not have to be an orderly cause to effect or syllogistic process. It can be the art of lingering on a subject. The noted English physicist, John Tyndall, called it "brooding." It is not daydreaming, although even this may be a kind of thinking: who can draw the line between daydreams and the visions of an artist? Daydreaming, however, is a random activity. The thinking you do when you jot down everything that comes to you has focus.

Your list of thoughts on how to quit smoking might look like this:

1. You can't taper off.
2. The after-breakfast cigarette—I cannot give it up.
3. And the cigarettes with coffee or cocktails.
4. Then, if you eat peanuts and candy instead of smoking cigarettes, you get fat.
5. Oh, but cigarettes are coffin nails.
6. How much better I felt when I did give it up: no fast pulse, no hoarse throat, no sore tongue, less jitteriness.
7. William James on habit; one cigarette undoes a week of abstinence.
8. When you quit, talk about it so that you are embarrassed if you start again.
9. But face it, it's all or nothing.
10. Choose a time to quit when the pressures are off—if there is such a time.

I could expand this list but it is now long enough to illustrate the thinking that goes on in this the first stage in the preparation of a speech. You might "brood" over the topic at many intervals over a period of several days or weeks, depending on the time you have. For a major speech some speakers consider one month a minimum for preparation. Do not overlook the subway or the Commuter's Special, the bus, or the lobby of a dentist's office—even the dentist's chair, if possible—as places where you can linger over your topic. Carry a notebook or note cards and unfailingly jot down whatever occurs to you, whatever you hear or see or read that is relevant.

You will be surprised at the amount of material you will gather if you are on the alert for the pertinent bit in the Here and Now. You overhear a conversation and someone says, "I can now truly say that I have no desire to smoke at all." A second person says, "My, but you have will power." "Rubbish," says the first person. "My doctor *ordered* me to stop." When you finally organize your material, you may not be able to use what you hear but you should write it down in case you can. The actual words of persons are often dramatic illustrative items.

Suppose you are looking at television and on comes one of those numerous cigarette commercials that are contrived with all the cunning of Madison Avenue and the motivational research people. You jot down some of the phrases. You then watch for other cigarette commercials. An important point is emerging for your speech: the task of quitting smoking is harder than ever what with all those images of sex and virility and the outdoor life cluttering up the screen. This is a point that you may not have thought of before, or if you did, it did not have the weight that it now has. It has acquired significance because you have been on the alert for anything that bears on your topic.

There is a source of material not utilized to the fullest and that is the press. Sure, you read a newspaper or two, a magazine or two, and you get some hazy ideas about a number of matters. But do you have the clipping habit? If not, cultivate it. Work out a filing system, not only for clippings but for your notes and anything else that may sooner or later have value in speechmaking. It is a common practice among ministers and lecturers to keep an elaborate filing system. "Most men," writes Ernest Dimnet in *The Art of Thinking*, "who have made a name in literature, politics or business have found it necessary to have a paper memory. . . ." The paper memory covers jottings, clippings, the notebook habit, and a filing system.

I do not go so far as to advise that you keep a diary or a journal, although one well versed in the processes of the creative mind, Arnold Bennett, does so advise. He favors the journal for it is less egoistic than the diary, more concerned with "the large spectacle of life." He tells of a man who kept a special journal devoted solely to current instances of superstition. The man did not have the slightest idea that "he was beginning a document of astounding interest and real scientific value; but such was the fact."

Journal or not, whatever you do to improve your paper memory is all to the good.

MAKE A TENTATIVE OUTLINE

Let us say that you have now accumulated a great deal of material, but it is in a disorganized state because you have not related it closely to points in an outline. The time has come to prepare a tentative outline. Your final outline will resemble the tentative one, but it will show differences in the supporting material for the various points. For as soon as you have done a tentative outline, you will find that you need to know more about certain points. This means, of course, some reading or research. Your final outline may also differ from the tentative one in that certain points or material—the minor points and weak or surplus material—will be omitted. The final outline will also include your introduction and your conclusion (see Chapter 6). And it will include more suggestions on what specifically you are going to say to the particular audience you are to address.

The tentative outline on "How to Stop Smoking," which is based on the list of jottings on the topic may look like this:

I. To stop smoking is hard.
    A. You can't taper off.
    B. Smoking is tied up with meals, coffee breaks, cocktails, and bridge.
    C. Television commercials constantly remind you of the pleasures of smoking.
II. But keep in mind the advantages of stopping.
    A. Fewer jitters.
    B. Less pounding of the heart and fast pulse.
    C. Less hoarseness and sore tongue.
    D. Less possibility of lung cancer; no coffin nails.
III. And you, we, *can* stop.
    A. Many people have quit—cite instances.
    B. Habits can be broken; smoking is just a habit.
        1. Cite William James and other psychologists on habit.
        2. First, you must really want to quit, feel that it is necessary.
        3. Second, you must remember that one cigarette undoes a week of abstinence.
    C. You can help yourself to quit.
        1. Talk about it so that you are under pressure to do it.
        2. Eat peanuts or candy when you feel the desire to smoke.
        3. Remember, one day at a time.
        4. Just two weeks, and each day will be easier.

This tentative outline suggests two phases in particular that you need to do some research on: (1) instances of people who have quit; (2) psychologists on habit.

YOU DO RESEARCH

In gathering material at this stage, you narrow the field. You set out to explore certain points; you look for certain data. Now you are after instances of people who have stopped smoking, and you want to find out what psychologists specifically say about habits, how to make or break them.

No matter what the topic, the sources of material are generally the same:

1. *Your own observation and experience.* I have already discussed this but I stress again the importance of what you yourself observe and experience.

2. *You write for information.* You write to persons or agencies who are authorities. A man was preparing a major speech on educational opportunities and facilities in the various states. He wrote to the departments of education of the states, and in a very short time he had reports and bulletins galore. Another man was to speak on selling insurance. He wrote to several insurance companies, who responded with letters and pamphlets. Another was to speak on how to direct a play. He wrote several "name" directors. To his surprise, most of them responded.

3. *You interview people.* What I have just said about writing for information goes for interviewing. But you need to be careful that you accurately record what you hear. You may have a portable tape recorder. The advantage of the interview over writing to a person is that you can cover more details of a subject.

4. *You read.* In speech preparation, read selectively, with particular purposes in mind. Read to find material for certain points; read to find certain kinds of material—statistics, testimony, cases. Read critically; just because something is in print does not make it accurate or authoritative. Even experts disagree. This is hard to put across to many people: print does not put a halo around opinion or supposed fact.

The business of research by reading covers a wide variety of media and reference guides: newspapers, magazines, bulletins, pamphlets, reports, books; indexes, yearbooks, guides to articles in magazines and newspapers; encyclopedias, dictionaries, who's who's. Here is a brief list of references to guide you:

For General Background
Encylopaedia Britannica
Encylopedia Americana
Textbooks

For Statistical Data
World Almanac
Information Please Almanac
Economic Almanac

Statistical Abstract
Government publications
Publications of industries, agencies, and organizations

Indexes to Periodicals
Reader's Guide to Periodical Literature
Industrial Arts Index
Public Affairs Information Service
Education Index
New York Times Index

Biographical Information
Who's Who
Who's Who in America
Who's Who in Commerce and Industry
Who's Who in Law
Who's Who among Physicians and Surgeons
Leaders in Education
Dictionary of American Biography

Special Helps
Bartlett's Familiar Quotations
Webster's Dictionary of Synonyms
Roget's International Thesaurus

YOU RECORD AND FILE MATERIAL

Do you want to be mentally efficient? Do you want to keep your intellectual house in good order? Then work out a system for recording and filing material. "Why go to all this trouble for speeches?" Answer: in the interests of intellectual honesty. This means that you use data carefully and accurately. Also, hearers respect the speaker who is careful with his material; respect is a powerful factor in attention and persuasion.

Prepare a bibliography. This is a systematic listing of the sources of your material. If you do this, you will not find yourself reading the same article again; if you are questioned you will be able to say that you have consulted such and such sources that support you; you will have the confidence of someone who is sure of his ground.

You can divide the bibliography as follows:

1. Books
2. Periodicals
3. Newspapers
4. Pamphlets, bulletins, reports
5. Letters
6. Interviews

You should identify accurately the entries under each division, as follows:

1. *Books.* Author, title, volume if more than one, publisher, place of publication, date.
2. *Periodicals.* Author, title of article, name of periodical, volume, date, page or pages.
3. *Newspapers.* Name of newspaper, author if indicated, title of article if given, date, page or pages.
4. *Pamphlets, bulletins, reports.* Author, title of subject, publisher, volume, date, pages if the publication carries more than one subject or includes more than one article on the same subject.
5. *Letters.* Author, date, place.
6. *Interviews.* Name of person interviewed, date, place.

WORK OUT A SYSTEM OF RECORDING DATA

I have mentioned the notebook as a valuable aid to the "paper memory." It is particularly useful as your ever-present partner in retaining what you come across in everyday life, in retaining also the striking phrases or sentences and sudden ideas that come to you. But there is also a method of recording data which is especially adapted to the additional research that you do. It is the method of recording on note cards, either the 3x5 or the 4x6 size. Such cards are convenient for speaking purposes; you can easily file them in a box and easily find them again; and they are the right size to use when you actually speak, much better than larger sheets of paper.

Now you are saying, "What is this! I thought this was a book on speech, not on paperwork. Carry a notebook, keep a journal, make out notecards! I give up!" You do have a point. There are many people successful in speechmaking and other intellectual pursuits who do not carry a notebook or keep a journal. There are few or none who do not have note cards or some other way of recording their research. If you wish, forget the notebook, forget the journal, but do take notes systematically.

It comes as a surprise to many people that effective speakers and writers go to great pains to keep track of their experience, their research, their ideas. Even genius does not flourish without discipline. Someone has said that genius is one-tenth talent and nine-tenths hard work. Someone else has said the genius is an infinite capacity for taking pains. The stress on hard work and taking pains oversimplifies what genius is but it also makes plain the necessity of discipline no matter the degree of talent.

Back to notecards then, or small memoranda paper, or what you will, just so that system is possible. These cards would be filed according to a scheme of headings. Each card would have a heading at the top, which would correspond with that on one of the index tabs in your file box or folder. You might have one or a hundred cards filed under a particular tab. Suppose on the topic, how to stop smoking, you work out such headings as: lung cancer, other physical effects, cigarette consumption, filters, TV commercials, psychology of habit. Each of these headings would be on a tab in your file.

A typical note card would read as follows:

FILTERS   EFFECTS

The National Tuberculosis Association reports: "No present method of treating tobacco or filtering the smoke has been proved to reduce the harmful effects of cigarette smoking; up to now, these harmful effects can be avoided only by *not* smoking cigarettes."

(Quoted in *New York Herald-Tribune* news article, May 6, 1960, p. 12).

Note that the heading *Filters* has a subhead. The more cards you file under a heading, the more the need for subheads so that you can efficiently find a particular card or cards. You may even want to label a separate tab *Effects*. This might be the case if you had started out with other subheads to *Filters* such as *Types* and *Advertising Value*. In fact, you may decide to eliminate the heading *Filters* because you have found so much material that you need a more definite scheme of classification. But do not concern yourself too much with this fineness of division. It is sufficient if you have a heading.

Here are other points about note cards to keep in mind:

1. Be sure to use quotation marks for quoted matter.
2. Be careful not to change the meaning when you put what you have read in your own words.
3. If you omit parts of a quotation, indicate omissions with three

periods, with four if the omission is at the end of a sentence, unless the sentence ends with a question mark or an exclamation point.

4. What you record on a single card should refer mainly to one point.
5. The source of the material on each card should be identified, as on the sample above. At the minimum, this means author, publication, date, and page. If the author or agency is unfamiliar, a statement about qualifications is necessary. Too often a speaker merely gives the name of a supposed authority who is unknown to his hearers.

3 YOU USE THE MATERIAL

STATISTICS

To CLARIFY, ILLUSTRATE, AND PROVE POINTS, YOU USE three kinds of data: statistics, examples, testimony. Your reasoning or logic is based on data. After I deal with data I shall take up reasoning. Note that here I do not consider persuasive materials as such; but keep in mind that persuasion in practice cannot be separated from data. Statistics can be as persuasive as appeals to self-preservation or love of country. For the sake of clearcut focus, however, I treat data separately.

You use statistics, even though you have heard that "there are lies, damn lies, and statistics." This saying makes us think about how such data should be gathered and used. The pollsters went wrong in the election of 1948 because they did not test opinion in the two weeks preceding election day. This was the period in which some six to eight million independent voters were making up their minds. This was the period in with the non-complacent Harry Truman out-talked the complacent Thomas Dewey. The pollsters had inaccurate samples. The results were statistical predictions that turned out to be worse than "damn lies," because they had the mask of mathematical accuracy. This is why statistics can be so villainous. They dress up error in the garb of the infallibility of numbers.

So test number one of statistics is: Is the sample accurate? Does it fully represent what you want to measure?

In *Time* magazine of December 14, 1959, an article in the Medicine section entitled "Smoking and Cancer (contd.)" began as follows: "From painstaking ten-minute to half-hour microscopic examinations of each of the 19,797 exquisitely thin slivers of tissue from human lungs, medical researchers reported last week that they had found the strongest anatomical evidence that heavy cigarette smoking is a potent cause of lung cancer." They found no cancer-type cells in the tissue of non-smokers or occasional smokers. But they found such cells in .3 per cent of the slivers of tissues of those who smoked "less than half a pack daily;

.8 per cent in the half-pack-to-a-pack-group; 4.3 per cent in the one-to-two packs group; and 11.4 per cent . . . from men smoking more than two packs." The conclusion seems warranted that smoking causes cancer. First, a very large number of slivers of tissue were examined. Second, the smokers were divided into five classes and the cancer-type cells arose, class by class, from 0 per cent to 11.4 per cent. Two tests of the accuracy of a sample are met: (1) a large enough number of specimens, (2) representative specimens, here five classes.

The statistics also meet another test. Experts made the findings and interpreted them. Two noted pathologists, Dr. Oscar Auerbach and Dr. Arthur Purdy Sout, excised and examined the slivers of tissue; two statisticians, Dr. E. Cuyler Hammond and Lawrence Garfinkel, both of the American Cancer Society, completed the team.

The worth of statistics may depend on why they were gathered. If the source is a government agency, which is supposedly competent and objective, or a private one like the Brookings Institute, renowned for its thorough research, or an education group that knows no master except the pursuit of truth, then one can be fairly certain that the findings are valid.

Even in academe, however, the objectivity of the source may be in question. Take the case of a study done by Professors Wiggins and Schoeck of Emory University on the attitudes of older people to federal support of medical care for them. The American Medical Association in a news release made much of the findings which were unfavorable to federal support. Professor Wayne E. Thompson, co-director of the Study of Occupational Retirement of Cornell University, wrote a letter to the *New York Times*, August 17, 1960, in which he was sharply critical of the Wiggins and Schoeck research. Charging that certain questions put to the older people were phrased to preclude a response favorable to federal medicine and that the sample of people questioned was weighted toward "relatively more affluent and vocal individuals," Professor Thompson stated that "in almost every respect the findings of the Wiggins and Schoeck study depart from those of other studies which have followed more vigorous sampling procedures." Professor Thompson also said that the study becomes "somewhat more understandable, given the information reported in *The Times* that he [Professor Wiggins] is a consultant to the AMA's medical economics department."

Therefore, do not be too ready to accept what you read or hear, no matter what the source.

FAULTS IN THE USE OF STATISTICS

A common fault in the use of statistics is to compare periods or groups that are not comparable. Statistics on juvenile delinquency in New York City for June, July, and August should not be compared with the same for March, April, and May, if the objective is to obtain a long view of increase or decrease. Delinquency rates are always up in the summer in New York City because school is out and children and youths have much idle time. It would be valid for the long view to compare the summer periods of the last five years. Similarly, unemployment figures for the winter months cannot be used to arrive at any conclusion concerning the state of the economy for the year unless they are compared to winter months of previous years. Nor can you validly infer that because Illinois, on the basis of public opinion polls, is going Democratic, Iowa will too. Illinois and Iowa are just not comparable; Chicago and Cook County with hefty voting power are consistently Democratic. And Illinois is not the concentrated agricultural state that Iowa is.

Another common fault in the use of statistics is to fail to define the unit measured. If you have figures on juvenile delinquency, make clear what the term means; in some cities, juvenile delinquency goes up to sixteen years of age, in others to eighteen. Again, it may include offenses only of the felony degree and serious misdemeanors. Or your statistic may include a calculation of "concealed" delinquency, the number of offenders not caught.

There are many terms in statistical reports which need careful definition, such as: *gross national product, consumer price index, disposable income, foreign aid, IQ, licensed drivers.* It is still possible in some states to get a driver's license without taking a written examinaton.

When you present statistical matter, be sure to relate it clearly to the point it is supposed to support. Do not leave it up to your hearers to draw the conclusion; it might be the wrong one. If you have figures that show the rising death rate from cancer over the last twenty years and you want to prove, not that we are worse off today from a health point of view, but that we are better off, be sure to make this clear. We are better off because more people live longer and cancer has more people to hit. Yet many hearers unless you made your point clear would form the opinion that we are worse off.

This is the day of the huge statistic. In an article, "Cipher Away!," in the *New York Times Magazine* of August 7, 1960, Frank Sullivan cautions of a "national peril"—"We are squandering our ciphers at a reckless pace. If we go on this way we may wake up one day and find ourselves without a cipher to our name." Sullivan had come across the statistic of our "gross national product," reported at $500,000,000,000, which to him was "not only gross, but obese and overstuffed." Add to this figure the announcements of the National Bureau of Standards that it has a clock in Boulder, Colorado, that ticks 9,200,000,000 ticks a second and of the National Safety Council that lightning strikes the earth 3,000,000,000 times a year, and you have a situation that threatens to drive Sullivan, and all of us, crazy.

What can be done to make huge statistics less stupefying? We can reduce them to practical terms. Even the amount of our gross national product makes some sense if we divide it by the population of the country, which would come to about $2,857 a person. Or make a graphic picture of the amount. Imagine it as broken up into ten dollar bills. Spread them over the surface of the United States—every inch would be covered! The famous agnostic lecturer of the last century, Robert G. Ingersoll, never forgot the picture drawn in his boyhood by a preacher of the length of time a bad boy would have to spend in hell: "Suppose that once in a billion years a bird should come from some far-off distant planet, and carry off in its little bill a grain of sand, a time would finally come when the last atom composing this earth would be carried away; and when this last atom was taken, it would not even be sunup in hell."

A large statistic should also be rounded off. A figure like $843,675,-438.65 is hard to listen to and harder to remember. Round it off to $843,000,000.

How many statistics should you use? It depends partly on the subject and purpose of your speech. Statistics need not be dull. But you can become so enmeshed in them that only a statistics buff could or would follow you. Err on the side of too few figures rather than on the side of too many.

Use large graphs and charts if there is any chance of confusion. Use them also for the sake of emphasis. A visual aid is a concrete illustration. And concreteness is one of the *musts* of a speaker.

Finally, it is never sufficient to say, "Statistics show that . . ." You must name the source.

AUDIO-VISUAL AIDS

Whenever your point lends itself to auditory or visual aids, use them. Audio-visual aids provide the utmost in concreteness. They can be graphic supplements of words. They include maps, diagrams, charts, pictures, slides, kinescopes, movies, disc and tape recordings.

In using such aids, take care to avoid the following faults:

1. *The aid not easily seen by all your hearers.* The picture or diagram may be too small; or you may concentrate on showing what you have only to those few who are up front; or if you are pointing to a map or to a diagram or chart on a blackboard, your body may cut off the view of a part of your audience.

2. *The distracting aid.* Do not distribute visual material for your hearers to pass around and examine while you are speaking. They will be distracted from what you say. Circulate the material before you speak; if possible, have enough so that every hearer has the material before him when you refer to it. Remember, do not talk to the map or to the blackboard; talk to the audience.

3. *The aid that gets out of hand.* Be sure you have the mechanics of your aid under control. See that roll-down maps stay down when they are supposed to. See that the sticker tape is in good condition. I remember a speaker who had gone to great pains to prepare a chart on a large sheet of construction paper. He arose and said a few words about the significance of the chart and then tried to tape it to the wood border just above the blackboard. But the tape wouldn't stick. He got one corner of the chart up but just as he secured the other corner, the first came loose; then just as he put the first up again, the other came loose; and so on, for a couple minutes, to the entertainment of the audience but the demoralization of the speaker.

   If you are to show slides or moving pictures, check lighting conditions, and projection equipment. The projector that throws a blurred image is worthless. A movie projector emits a low continuous noise that can mask your words unless you speak loudly.

4. *The aid that is too detailed.* A congested chart is no aid at all. If it is not readily grasped, you would be better off using words alone. The too detailed chart is also usually the one with words and symbols too small; everything is squeezed together. The chart itself should have broad strokes, major stresses; you can supply details when you explain it.

USE TESTIMONY OR AUTHORITY

The use of testimony ranges from what Grandma says about what Miracle Liver Pills have done for her to what a scientist or a scholar or an agency says about a thing within his or its special ken. Not that Grandma is necessarily the least dependable of the witnesses; she is but the humblest of them and what she says may not get into a newspaper or a journal. But as to the liver pills, she may know whereof she speaks.

We have seen that the worth of statistics may depend on the source. Does the source, or authority, have some personal or business interest which might influence his research or his views? If a famous baseball player endorses Sweeteen chewing gum, does he do so purely because he likes it? If a Hollywood actress holds in her delicate hands a bar of Lovely soap, does she do so in a selfless desire to share a beauty boon? Testimonials have long been a staple of advertising. Remember the white-jacketed, world-renowned, Viennese specialists who spoke for yeast or aspirin or gelatine cubes? See today the rugged, outdoor cigarette men, and the healthy, wholesome beer girls.

But such testimonials help sell products. They increase the appeal and prestige of products. They may not prove the merit of products, but what is proof, after all, amid competing, often conflicting, claims? Proof is what convinces.

Suppose you set out to prove that desegregation has made marked progress in the South. You have amassed data including much testimony. Imagine that you are to speak on the subject to three audiences: (1) a PTA in Nashville, Tennessee; (2) a Rotary Club in Atlanta, Georgia; (3) a League of Women Voters Club in Hartford, Connecticut. Assume that the audience most resistant to your thesis would be the Rotary Club of Atlanta, that the PTA of Nashville, a city known for its moderation on the question, would be critical but fairly receptive, and that the League of Women Voters of Hartford would be sympathetic.

The question is: Would proof for your proposition be the same for all three audiences (*proof* now defined as evidence that convinces)? Put the question this way: Would that which convinces in Hartford also convince in Nashville and Atlanta? The answer, obviously, is *No*. You would not need in Hartford the mass of testimony and documented cases which you would need in critical but receptive Nashville. But how about Atlanta? Would the problem of persuasion be solved by data? In Atlanta you would be up against the Deep South bias. You would be better off in Atlanta if you took the line that, while you and your listeners might not like the way things were going, you might as well make the best of it. If you had enough humor and camaraderie before that Atlanta Rotary Club, you might even get them to accept your notions that it is perfectly possible to eat with Negroes in restaurants, ride with them in buses, and go to school with them. If this happens, then you have proved indeed that desegregation has made progress in the South.

Thus proof is not simply having sufficient data. Proof is a human thing, and, therefore, a most variable commodity.

We tend to believe what we want to believe. Most members of the American Medical Association are quite receptive to the official position on federal medical insurance for the aged. Members of the WCTU are sympathetic to the outpourings of teetotalers. Professors in the sciences listen with relish to educators who animadvert on the inexact humanities. And behold, members of the United States Supreme Court, this most judicial of bodies, where bias is supposedly at a minimum, often go their own way and dissent from the majority opinion.

Since bias is common, we have to be careful in the choice of authority. One way to antagonize a group is to use testimony which, though expert, it cannot stomach. Walter Reuther on the need for a guaranteed annual minimum wage for the United Auto Workers might be hard for the stockholders of General Motors to swallow.

If up to now I have seemed to neglect competence itself as a test of authority, it is not that I hold it of little importance. In fact, I would put it first in any listing of the tests of authority in order of importance:

1. Is the authority competent? Can he see and hear? Is he of sound mind? Is he an expert? Has he had firsthand access to the facts?

2. Is the authority biased? Does his position, wealth, place of residence, his age or connection with an agency (or other factors) render his testimony suspect?

3. Is the authority acceptable? What is his reputation? Will a given audience accept him? Because of the climate of opinion, an authority may be competent and unbiased and yet inacceptable.

4. Is the authority supported by other authorities? A single authority in support of a controversial view carries little weight. Several authorities who agree increase the presumption of truth.

In presenting authority, remember these essentials:

1. Show that he is qualified, if he is unknown to your hearers. Say something about his position, his experience.

2. Identify accurately the publication or medium in which your authority testifies. Do not say: "I read in the paper the other day—let me see, what day was it, I think it was Thursday—that someone said—I think it was John Doe. No, it wasn't, it was——Oh, well . . ." Give the

title (if a publication) and the date; you should give volume and page if exact documentation is necessary; you should be ready with volume and page in case you are challenged. If you are using the authority as he spoke on television or radio, name the program and the date.

3. State accurately what your authority has said. Never quote out of context. Do not do what promoters of plays and books often do; they quote in their advertisements only the laudatory remarks of reviewers. The review on the whole may be unfavorable.

When you do not quote the exact words of an authority but state the gist of the words, be sure that you do not distort or misrepresent.

4. Don't quote too much. A series of quotations does not make a speech. Do not let quotations replace your own thinking and your own words. Authorities support you; they should not take your place.

5. Another drawback in quoting too much is that it compells you to read too much; your eyes are on your notes; you lack direct contact with your hearers.

Now what of the words of the seer or the poet? If we want to quote from Robert Frost—"Something there is that doesn't love a wall,"—are we to ask whether he had access to the facts, or whether he is prejudiced? Proverbs, epigrams, lines of poetry, all etch truths. If they come from the Bible, from Pascal or Benjamin Franklin, from Shelley or T. S. Eliot, shall we bring to bear upon their authors the tests of the world that is too much with us? No, you cannot apply systematic tests to this class of authority; their truth is too personal.

EXAMPLES: MAKE YOUR IDEAS CONCRETE

"Hot air" is the vocalization of vagueness. It is agitation in a vacuum. The hot-air vendor loves the tried and true generalities. He shuns the concrete example, the specific case.

"It is the business of an orator," says an old Oriental proverb, "to turn the ears of an audience into eyes." An orator, a speaker, is in this respect like a poet. The poet is a maker of images. His insights, his ideas, come out as images. The insights and ideas of a speaker should also come out as images.

Help your hearers to see and hear and otherwise sense an idea. In his essay on style, English philosopher Herbert Spencer declares that the concrete not only sets forth a matter in practical terms, but also makes for "economy of attention," which means that one gets the point with a minimum of effort.

Make it easy for your hearers to get the point. Make it easier for yourself to get their attention. Do what is done in this excerpt from a power-ful speech, "The Year of the Rat," delivered by Charles H. Brower, president of the Batten, Barton, Durstine and Osborne advertising agency, to the Advertising Federation of America in Boston on Febru-ary 9, 1960:

I have said that inflation is a disease of the American spinal column. What I have not said is that almost all of our troubles come as a result of the same disease. The disease might be called Epidemic Cynical Selfishness—it is the healthy cells or rugged individualism gone wild.

Epidemic Cynical Selfishness. Or E.C.S. It might be called "ME-FIRST-ITIS," or "MAKE WAY FOR NUMBER ONE," or "WHAT'S IN IT FOR ME?," or "GOOD GUYS FINISH LAST," and it is about as far away from the Golden Rule as it is possible to get.

Russell Conwell's "Acres of Diamonds" was full of practical, pictorial, dramatic matter, like the following:

But your wealth is too near. I was speaking in New Britain, Connecticut, on this very subject. There sat five or six rows from me a lady. I noticed the lady at the time, from the color of her bonnet. I said to them, what I say to you now, "Your wealth is too near to you! You are looking right over it!" She went home after the lecture and tried to take off her collar. The button stuck in the buttonhole. She twisted and tugged and pulled and finally broke it out of the buttonhole and threw it away. She said: "I wonder why they don't make decent collar buttons?"

He husband said to her: "After what Conwell said tonight, why don't you get up a collar button yourself? Did he not say that if you need anything other people need it; so if you need a collar button there are millions of people needing it. Get up a collar button and get rich. 'Wherever there is need there is a fortune.' "

Then she made up her mind to do it; and when a woman makes up her mind, and doesn't say anything about it, she does it! And she invented this "snap button," a kind of a button that snaps together from two pieces, through the buttonhole. That very woman can now go over the sea every summer in her own yacht and take her husband with her. And if he were dead she would have enough money left to buy a foreign count or duke, or some such thing.

A lecture of today, "How to Live with Yourself," by Dr. Murray Banks, published in *McCall's*, March, 1960, is the equal of "Acres of Diamonds" in popular appeal. Dr. Banks has delivered it over five thou-sand times. It abounds in the concrete, the graphic, the lively. For in-stance:

Why do people convert their fears: Why do people convert their fears into bodily disturbance? To understand this, you would have to look into the home life of a child to see how he learns his particular adjustment to his daily problems. Let us look into the home of Little Joe, age ten. He gets up one morning, eats a hearty breakfast and on the way to school, he suddenly remembers he has an arithmetic test to take. He thinks. Maybe I should throw up. Then I wouldn't have to take the test. But he manages to keep it down. In the classroom, you can observe him doing the arithmetic problems; but the third problem is too difficult for him—so up it comes.

The principal sends him home. Mama puts him to bed. Papa buys him a toy. Sister reads him a story. Why, the upset stomach has had a high value! He has saved face.

If he had come home with a mark of 50 on his test, what would Mama have said? "Why are you so stupid? Why can't you be smart, like the little boy next door?" In this case, however, she says, "Imagine how smart my little Joe must be. Even though he was sick, he managed to get fifty. Can you imagine what he would have got if he hadn't been sick?"

Now Little Joe is Big Joe, and whenever he meets a problem that is too much for him, he throws up without even thinking about it. He goes from doctor to doctor, complaining of a nervous stomach. But can't you see that his nervous stomach is a protection? A protection from the truth, which is: "Joe you're a flop." With his nervous stomach, he says to the world. "World, look at me. World, I could be such a success. I'm really quite brilliant. But my nervous stomach, that's what prevents me." And Joe would rather suffer from all the misery of the stomach disorder than face the truth—that he is a failure.

Note in the excerpt that the little boy is named. He is Little Joe, age ten. He does specific things. He has specific feelings and thoughts. Mama uses actual words. The Little Joe becomes Big Joe, who is as specific as Little Joe.

Elsewhere in the speech, to illustrate the point that knowledge pays off, Dr. Banks says:

In a large industrial plant, one of the machines broke down. All work had to be stopped. An expert was called to repair the machine. The expert came and, with a little hammer, tapped here and tapped there. Finally, he announced that the machine was ready to operate.

Later, a bill arrived from the expert. It stated: "For services rendered, $200." A clerk in the accounting department sent back the bill and asked for "an itemized statement of services rendered." Back came the bill: "Itemized statement for services rendered: For tapping power machine, $1. For knowing where to tap, $199."

The humorous touch is frequent in the speech.

> Yet isn't it strange that there are "none so blind as they that won't see?"
> A Professor was attempting to illustrate to his class the effects of alcohol on the human body. He placed a worm in a glass of water, and the worm crawled out. He then placed the worm in a glass of alcohol, and it was killed. "What's the moral?" asked the Professor.
> A student said, "If you drink alcohol, you never have worms."

A final example:

> Beware of feeling too important. Remember there is always someone who feels more important than you do. In a hospital for the mentally ill, a patient sat in grandiose pose. A psychiatrist, passing by, said to him, "Who do you think you are?"
> "I, sir," answered the patient, "am Napoleon."
> "Who told you you were Napoleon?"
> "God told me."
> A voice came from the next bed: "I did not."

It is the sustained use of the actual and the graphic, eddying with humor and fused with sense and substance, that makes "How to Live with Yourself" a masterpiece.

THE USE OF HUMOR

Thomas Corwin, the best stump speaker who ever "came down the pike," was renowned for his wit and funny stories. Yet he once said to President Garfield that "it was the greatest mistake of his life that he ever cracked a joke or made a funny speech for people would never believe that a funny man could have any solid abilities. . . ." Corwin's own political career, however, belied any such distrust of him. In forty years, 1821–1861, the people of Ohio repeatedly elected him to public office: the state legislature, the national House of Representatives, the governorship, the United States Senate. Nor did Abraham Lincoln's well-known talents in humor keep him from the highest office, although they did draw criticism. It was not Adlai Stevenson's penchant for witty remarks that kept him from the presidency; it was the overwhelming popularity of his opponent. Yet in a close election, who knows? It might be the workings of the Law of Political Gravity—formulated by Clayton Fritchie in the *New York Times Magazine*, July 3, 1960—that would make the difference: "Humor is okay; wit can be dangerous; wisecracking is disastrous."

Humor can give pith and pungency to ideas. It can dissipate tensions and diminish resistance. If you are engaged in a heated discussion, a funny anecdote or witty retort can raise the boiling point. While too much humor can spoil the broth, none at all can congeal it.

Perhaps a distinction should be made between humor and wit. If humor is of the heart and wit of the mind, a little of the latter to certain audiences might be too much—"He's an egghead."

The new "sick-sick" humor, which is that of a sour heart and a sharp mind, is all right for a night club or a coffee house, a beatnik hangout or even a television show, but it is of little value for practical speechmaking. It is too bitter for the average taste. I cannot imagine a situation for a regular speech that would allow the speaker, à la "sick-sick," to tell of a moronic American commander of a Polaris submarine who gave orders to fire on Miami Beach, or of a suggestion to Abraham Lincoln—"If you can't find another couple for bridge, why not go to a play with your wife?"—and then to tell of someone saying, "Outside of that, Mrs. Lincoln, how did you enjoy the show?"

As in other aspects of speechmaking, it is speaker, purpose, occasion, and audience that should determine the humor and wit in a speech. I confess to being uncomfortable whenever a minister in his sermon tries to amuse. Again, I may appreciate the risqué in a speech but I object to the smutty. Of course what I regard as risqué, someone else might consider smutty and vice versa. I do not object to the bit about the housewife who flung up her window and asked the milkman, "Do you have the time?" Nor do I object to the story, as told by Max Eastman, of the woman who boarded a train with nine children, and when the conductor came for the tickets she said: "Now these three are thirteen years old and pay full fare, but those over there are only six, and these three here four and a half." The conductor looked at her in astonishment.

"Do you mean to say you get three every time?" he asked. "Oh, no," she said. "Sometimes we don't get any at all."

When in doubt about the propriety of humor, don't use it.

An interesting question arises: May a speaker ridicule others? The art of belittlement and defamation has a long and honorable history, from Demosthenes to Winston Churchill. It is a phase of what Aristotle calls ethical proof. Ancient Greek and Roman orators and teachers of oratory studied ways to enhance ethical proof, that is, the impact of personality and character in speaking. One way was to run down an opponent. Belittle him. Bring him into disrepute. By so doing, if you do it well, you also elevate yourself.

The British have always been adept in the art of belittlement. It is a staple of their oratory. During the parliamentary election campaign in the fall of 1959, these were a few of the bright spots:

LORD HAILSHAM: "I did not criticize Mr. Gaitskell's war record. I merely pointed out, quite factually and calmly, that it was quite as democratic for the Prime Minister to have gone to Eton and joined the Guards as it was for Mr. Gaitskell to have gone to Winchester and joined the Ministry of Economic Warfare."

PRIME MINISTER MACMILLAN: "Mr. Bevan [Aneurin Bevan, Labor party foreign affairs spokesman] once described Mr. Gaitskell as a desiccated calculating machine. That is only a half-truth. I still think he is rather desiccated, but his reputation as a calculator has gone with the wind."

MR. GAITSKELL: "Mr. Macmillan is a pretty peculiar schoolmaster. He asks questions, but he will not or cannot answer questions himself."

RICHARD A. BUTLER: Home Secretary in the Conservative Cabinet: "The slogan of the Socialist [Labor] party is 'a bribe a day keeps the Tories away.' That will be shown up by the electorate as an utterly unsound method of governing our affairs."

LADY VIOLET BONHAM CARTER, of the Liberal party: "Mr. Macmillan's speeches are one long cock-a-doodle-do of self-congratulations."

No one can beat Winston Churchill at verbal cut and thrust. Of the Chamberlain government, he said: "They are decided only to be undecided, resolved to be irresolute, adamant for drift, all-powerful for impotence." Of Clement Attlee: "A modest man but then he has so much to be modest about." Of Sir Stafford Cripps: "There, but for the grace of God, goes God."

Although Americans preach sportsmanship, eschew sarcasm, and frown upon mudslinging, we are not slouches at belittlement. Wendell Willkie was called the "barefoot boy from Wall Street," and no one knows how much damage the phrase did him. When Thomas E. Dewey was nominated for President in 1944, he was said by Alice Longworth to be "the bridegroom on the wedding cake." Politicians estimated the damage as considerable. Senator Kerr of Oklahoma said, in 1952, that Eisenhower was "the greatest living unknown soldier." In 1960 no one was in doubt about the target of the admonition, "Don't send a boy to do a man's work."

A speaker may ridicule others. But he must do it with finesse and not too much. And he must know when to do it. This advice is easy to give; the use of it depends on one's talents and seasoning. There are some people who will shun the advice for the good reason that they do not like to belittle others.

4 BE LOGICAL

BE LOGICAL. THIS IS EASY TO SAY, HARD TO DO. ONE MAN'S
logic is another man's illogic—"Rising wages cause inflation," "Democratic administrations lead to war," "Republican administrations result
in depressions." Or a woman's logic is a man's illogic—"Dick, I need
that dress because I have these gloves." Or vice versa—"You know,
Honey, the doctor said I ought to walk more, so I'm going to get that
set of matched woods I've been talking about." Again, the logic of one
time is the illogic of another—"Sir, the particular prominences of your
cranial structure are indubitable evidences of high intellection combined
with extraordinary amativeness."

The state of one's logic depends greatly on the state of one's ignorance. In general, the less the ignorance, the more the logic—in general,
but not necessarily; the more some people know, the more they go
wrong. A distinguished but hard-bitten and cynical geologist once told
me that "the primary value of a college education was to give people
more reasons to believe as they want to believe." I do not hold with this
crabbed doctrine, but there are the "educated" who gleen from the passing days only such facts as fit their bents.

Knowledge, however, is still a number one safeguard against illogic.
We read, for instance, that juvenile delinquency is on the increase in
families of middle income. We also read, in Paul Goodman's book,
Growing Up Absurd, that the lack of a sense of vocation, of working at
something that counts, results among the young in frustration and devil-
try. We read in that book that the very system that breeds organization
men, in which the job itself counts for little, is the one that breeds young
offenders. We get a new perspective on the problem: we are no longer
so sure that the main causes of juvenile delinquency are poverty and
pigmentation. Our logic has taken on another dimension. We have es-
caped an elementary lapse of logic, omitting from the analysis of a
problem a major cause.

As potent as ignorance in illogical thinking is a bent to make facts toe the line. The usual parent thinks the daubings of his six-year-old the signs of creative genius; the art teacher is less appreciative. If you like someone, what he does is all right; if you dislike him, what he does is all wrong. You can "get something on" anybody if you look hard enough or wait long enough.

Factual distortion or selectivity, like sin, death, and taxes, has its lighter side—if we are not instantly involved. In the 1880's a controversy arose among the Norwegian immigrants in South Dakota concerning the substitution of English for Norwegian in the Lutheran Church services. As children came and grew, the issue became explosive, threatening to rend communities into language sects. At one meeting an old immigrant, speaking in Norwegian, delivered a memorable denunciation of the supporters of English services. His final, climactic statement, translated, was: "If the Norwegian language was good enough for Jesus Christ, it is good enough for me."

Objectivity is not easy to come by. How does it happen that the United States Supreme Court has many 5 to 4 and 6 to 3 decisions? The judges have before them the same set of facts; they listen to the same legal arguments; they read the same briefs. Why the split decisions? Because judges too are human. They differ in economic, political, and religious backgrounds; they differ in intelligence, education, imagination, and temperament. Some of you remember the "ornery" Supreme Court that declared the National Recovery Act and other measures of the New Deal unconstitutional. President Roosevelt set out to change all that, to "pack the court," his critics said, by enlarging it. He did not succeed, and great was the triumph of the *Chicago Tribune* in announcing the failure in huge headlines, "Dictatorship Bill Defeated!" But President Roosevelt was convinced that the court was partial to "economic royalists." Perhaps Justice Felix Frankfurter also has in mind the Supreme Court when he says in his recent book, *Felix Frankfurter Reminisces*: "You damned sociologists, you historians who want to get it all nice and fine on paper, you haven't learned how much in this world is determined by non-syllogistic reasoning."

We all have a bent to distort, or select, facts. Call it bias, call it prejudice, we all have it, on any question. But if we are aware of its omnipresence, we can check its outrages. If you know how hard it is to think objectively, and why, you'll be closer to logic than most people.

A third powerful factor in illogical, or logical, thinking is the word. And this calls for a separate section.

WORDS THAT HINDER CLEAR THINKING

We think *with* words and react *to* words. Words are a form of human behavior.

Words that hinder clear thinking and sensible behavior can be classified as follows:

1. Fuzzy words
2. Highfalutin words
3. Fighting words
4. Scary words
5. Souped-up words
6. Tricky words

1. *Fuzzy* words. *Fuzzy* covers a lot of ground. It may mean abstract words, like *love, justice, truth, socialism, democracy*. An abstract word has as many shades of meaning as there are individuals in your audience. Can you use the words then? Of course, you can. But you should be mindful of the possibilities of misunderstanding. When you use such words, make clear the sense in which you are using them. While you cannot ever make a word mean to someone else exactly what it means to you, you can get closer to mutual understanding by defining the word when you use it. Again, however, don't go too far. If you want to say to someone, "I love you," you need not also say, "*Love*, as I now use the term, means intellectual, spiritual, and physical attraction."

Fuzzy here also refers to clichés. Maybe 1984 is earlier than we think. In the George Orwell novel, *1984*, "Newspeak," an official jargon "designed not to extend but to diminish the range of thought," rules men's minds. Thinking is a manipulation of clichés. Are we not close to a like predicament?

A powerful cliché today is "the separation of church and state." With it you can rout all but the doughtiest supporters of federal loans to parochial schools. The only enemy of the cliché is fact, but fact can do little to dispel the incantation of "the separation of church and state." Even if an advocate of federal loans to parochial schools were to quote Justice Douglas of the United States Supreme Court ("The First Amendment, however, does not say that in every and all respects there shall be a separation of church and state.")—or were to point to the prayers in legislative halls, the proclamations making Thanksgiving Day a holiday, the "So help me God" in courtroom oaths, the tax exemptions for church property, the beneficiaries under the "GI Bill of Rights" who attend church colleges—even armed with all these facts, an advocate of federal loans to parochial schools would have hard going against "the separation of church and state."

Equally potent is "socialized medicine." Let us suppose that you are discussing a proposal of federal health insurance for the aged through the social security system. If you are against the proposal, all you need to do to cast a spell over most listeners is to ring the changes on "socialized medicine." Go to the American Medical Association. Quote the *AMA News* of March 20, 1961, as follows: "The Socialist party in the United States has launched a nation-wide campaign for socialized medicine in America and has made it clear it supports President Kennedy's proposal for health and medical care through the Social Security system as the vehicle with which to bring full-blown socialized medicine to this country." Note the repetition: "Socialist," "socialized," "Social," "socialized."

Or take "Madison Avenue"—which now stands charged with all the corruptions of American culture. Because of Madison Avenue we are liars, adulterers, cheaters, and drunkards! As a whipping boy, Madison Avenue has superseded Wall Street.

Who would have thought that two such fine words as *progressive* and *education* could form a cliché that means spoiled brats, bad grammar, and Johnny can't read. But "Progressive Education" means just that.

If someone attributes juvenile delinquency to the emphasis on violence in comic books, television shows, and movies—but you wish to absolve these media—just blame "Progressive Education."

And what of those standbys among clichés, "liberal" and "conservative"? How their meaning has changed! A liberal today is a different kind of animal than he was in the days of the New Deal. In the thirties he crusaded for food, clothing, and shelter at any price. Now, in a land of plenty, if he crusades at all, it is for freedom from international anarchy and for freedom from racial discrimination at home and abroad.

The term, "conservative," in New Deal days was a bad word. It stood for Wall Street, for Hoover Republicans, for stuffed-shirtism. Today it stands for those who would conserve our original freedoms and our faith in man-made but divinely ordered law and institutions. Except for the McKinley conservatism of Senator Barry Goldwater, a conservative can be as indistinguishable from a liberal as a New Republican is from a New Frontiersman.

As "New Deal" became a stigmatic cliché and, as "New Republicanism" fell into disrepute, so, I predict, will the "New Frontier." It takes at least a four-year term for a political slogan to decline to an ignominious cliché.

2. *Highfalutin* words. These words are closely related to the fuzzy ones but they are on a higher level, or in a specialized category, of obfuscation.

The law has always enjoyed renown for its gobbledegook. In protest against legalese the late John B. Kelly, father of Princess Grace of Monaco, decided to write his own will. "Kids will be called 'kids' and not 'issue,' and it will not be cluttered up with 'parties of the first part,' 'per stirpes,' 'perpetuities' . . . and a lot of other terms that I am sure are only used to confuse those for whose benefit it was written."

Ambiguity is plentiful in politics. The seasoned politician avoids clarity. "When a politician gives his own opinions," writes Simson Bullitt in his book, *To Be A Politician,* "he shuns exactitude. His words have rounded edges, for he knows he may be understood." Or as the seasoned Senator Everett Dirksen of Illinois put it, in describing what a colleague had said in reply to an embarrassing question: "Well, at that point he shouldn't have said anything, and that's precisely what he did."

Word troubles abound in international jargon. Take the word, *aggression,* popular at the United Nations. Special committees appointed in 1953 and 1956 to define the term adjourned without agreement. In 1959 another special committee set up to decide when the General Assembly should discuss the problem postponed decision even on the procedural question until 1962. The secretary of the committee remarked that the meaning of *aggression* "grows more and more obscure." The simple definition that aggression is the use of force by one nation against another is to the Soviet Union a "mere repetition of elementary truths." The "enumerative" definition of the Soviet which goes into economic, "indirect," and ideological considerations is to the Western nations a source of "mischief and confusion." It is a good bet that no official definition will ever materialize.

The various senses of *democracy* in international usage force the conclusion that everyone believes in it but nobody understands it. A definition of hypocrisy comes to mind, that it is the homage that vice pays to virtue. At the United Nations someone from Pakistan, which has at best a benevolent despotism, speaks of his country's "controlled democracy." Someone from Czechoslavakia, which has a government both unpopular and undemocratic, speaks of his country's "popular democracy." Someone from Indonesia speaks of "guided democracy," which means either tyranny or chaos. Then there is the "People's Democracy" of Communist China. And the King of Nepal bans political parties "to help the suitable growth of democracy."

Neutrality in world parlance has interesting synonyms: "positive neutralism," "active independence," "non-alignment," "disengagement." None of them appears to alter the question: Whom are you neutral for or against?

Peace, of course, now means cold war and just about everybody seems willing to settle for this equivocation.

One of the most fertile domestic sources of obscurity is, of all places, the halls of academe. The professorial mind seems to have an antipathy to simplicity and clarity. John L. Lewis missed his calling, he who could say, "I wish to disaffiliate myself from any association with this enterprise." He would have been right at home in departments of education, sociology, psychology, and communication.

Educationists luxuriate in such phrases as: "optimal ratio of variety and homogeneity," "underprivileged preadolescent," "enrichment both horizontal and vertical," "Pupil-Pupil Intervisitation: An Integrative Experience." Sociologists are even more adept at polysyllabic confusion. Only a sociologist could have composed the following excerpt, from a study of a group of colleges: "These subcultures (of types of student orientation) are fluid systems of norms and values which overlap and flow into one another on any particular campus in ways that challenge the effort to distinguish them analytically. Yet that effort, for all the violence it does to the complexity of social life, appears justified by the congruence of these types with observed reality, and by the light it sheds not only on student subcultures themselves, but on colleges as social organizations embedded in a larger social structure." Even so clear-headed a sociologist as David Reisman can write: ". . . the private and sheltered person too can find in politics a way of acculturation to the gamut of cultures which our society still encapsulates. . . ."

The murky vocabulary of psychology is well known, no point in going into it here, but it comes as a shock to find that obscurity has invaded fields where clarity once held sway, English and communications. A committee of academians of the Modern Language Association, no less, came up with the following in a report on the teaching of English: "The values of the literary component of English are sequential and incremental. They reside in enlargement of the mind by an experience of discovery and recognition, new discovery and association based upon increased recognition."

Recently a new Division of Communications was established at a large Western university. The announcement of its opening declared: "The existence of free and effective channels of communication among men is a basic requisite to an informed public consensus upon the important issues of society which, in turn, is essential to the viability of our democratic form of government." (Translation: Effective communication insures the knowledge essential to strong democratic government.) The announcement went on: "The ability to recognize the techniques of communication provided by the technology of our age for the clear and rapid dissemination of information and the ability to draw upon the scholarship and arts of our institutions of higher education to reduce the incidence of semantic ambiguity and demagogic device require the existence of a skilled and educated profession of communications." (Translation: To develop abilities to evaluate the techniques and devices of modern communication requires a profession of communications.)

The future of clarity seems dark. John Crosby, the columnist, predicts that "the date on which language will become totally unintelligible, when, in short, obscurity becomes total blackness, is 2086." Says he, "I'll be dead then, thank God."

3. *Fighting* words. These words arouse a wide range of ill feeling, from the passive annoyance of an individual to the militant wrath of nations. J. Edgar Hoover resents being called "the nation's top cop." He objects to "cop." He wrote to Dr. Bergen Evans, then moderator of the television program, *The Last Word*: "As a career law-enforcement officer, I abhor the word 'cop' in reference to members of our profession. The expression is degrading to law enforcement. . . . holds the same unsavory connotation as 'quack' and 'hack' when referring to the doctor and the journalist." Dr. Evans supports Hoover, saying that "cop" is an underworld word. John Lardner, however, points out in the *New Yorker*, July 18, 1959, that "the most relentless users of the word are cops. . . . 'He's a real cop,' 'He's a good cop,' 'I've been on the cops for twenty years,' 'Claffey is a hell of a cop,' 'What kind of cop would I be if I let you drive like that?' " Whether Hoover and Evans can reform the cops remains to be seen.

Then there was the fracas involving Clare Boothe Luce and Senator Wayne Morse, that began April 28, 1959, the date the Senate was to vote on Mrs. Luce's nomination as ambassador to Brazil. It was believed that approval was certain, even after the three-hour attack of Senator Morse who charged that in past political campaigns she had been "subversive . . . sinister . . . hysterical." These were fighting words and Mrs. Luce, no slouch herself in name-calling, was equal to the situation. When she heard that she had been confirmed as ambassador to Brazil by a 79 to 11 vote, she said for the press: "I am grateful for the overwhelming vote of confirmation in the Senate. We must now wait until the dirt settles. My difficulties, of course, go some years back and began when Senator Wayne Morse was kicked in the head by a horse."

Senator Morse read the news release to the Senate, which proved, he said, that "this slanderer" was not fit for the office because of "her complete lack of tact and diplomacy." Senate anger arose over this insult to one of their members.

Several senators stated that they regretted their votes to confirm. The mellifluous Everett Dirksen failed in pacification attempts. Mr. Luce jumped into the fray, condemned Morse's "vitriolic" attacks, and advised his wife to resign. She did resign. The lesson? "Sticks and stones may break my bones." And words can hurt me, too.

4. *Scary* words. These words and fighting words are often indistinguishable. It may be the scariness of a word that arouses, in self-defense, belligerence. "Annihilation" in the news bulletins of the propaganda ministry of Nazi Germany was calculated to strike terror into the hearts of the enemy and for a while it succeeded too well. If at first it increased defiance, its repetition numbed a foe.

A hospital once put on the door to a section the words "Tumor Clinic." It aroused so much anxiety and fright that it was eliminated.

Scary words have their place. But we are here concerned with them when they interfere with clear thinking. "Danger! Sharp Curve!" is an effective warning, but the indiscriminate use of such words invites curious reactions. Dr. Seymour Feshback, a psychiatrist at the University of Pennsylvania, says in the *New York Times*, May 2, 1959: "You're not going to get many persons to go in for a cancer examination with signs saying, 'You (in big red letters) may be one of those who will die of cancer this year.' " It will be much more effective if you offer objective data and calm, easy to act upon, advice. Again, if you stress the horrors of automobile accidents, many people will simply tune out the scare messages because they cannot accept them. It would be better to increase the appeal of safety belts or to stress traffic caution as a responsibility of good citizenship.

The main cause of stuttering, according to Professor Wendell Johnson of the State University of Iowa, lies in the misuse of the word "stuttering." An overanxious mother hears her child repeat a sound or a word several times. "Oh, Johnny," she says, "You're stuttering. Quit it." Johnny may react in two ways. Either he will capitalize upon repetition as a technique of gaining attention or he will be so wrought up over the distress of his mother that he will be driven to repeat more than ever. Then mama gets more distressed, and Johnny does, too. And so it goes, from that which is normal, namely, repetition of sounds and words in the early years, to that which is abnormal, stuttering. The main factor in the distress of both Johnny and his mother was fear. Mother's fear infected Johnny. Professor Johnson and his followers say that the real patient who comes to the speech clinic with Johnny is not Johnny but his mother.

5. *Souped-up* words. Look in any general family magazine. There will be all kinds of superlatives, like the following:

(a) "Maybelline specializes *exclusively* in everything to make eyes beautiful."
(b) "The best taste yet in a filter cigarette."
(c) "101 glorious ways to cook chicken."
(d) "A single tablet takes care of nature's tardiness."
(e) "*The* toothbrush that won't pass germs along."
(f) "*Your all day* veil of fragrance."
(g) "Put the finest label on your table."
(h) "Cast a magic spell."
(i) "Perfume your psyche—It's a whole new way to relax."

When you get around to buying the best or the finest or the greatest of everything and you use advertising as your guide, you had better build a huge storage place because you will have bought something of everything.

On the level of everyday exchange of words, how about such superlatives as *fantastic, marvelous, wonderful, fabulous, superb, stunning, terrible, awful*? How often do we use such words? By the frequency of our use, we can measure the carelessness of our thought. Is the gasoline consumption of a car ever fabulous? Is a lipstick ever marvelous? Sometimes, but rarely, such words would be accurate. If you stood at the summit of Pike's Peak on a day of clear visibility and gazed at the vast expanse of country below, you might quite properly use the word *wonderful*. Or if you landed on the moon and encountered creatures with huge bald heads, with eyes fore and aft but no ears, with long skinny arms and short fat legs, you could use without exaggeration the word *fantastic*.

We have all heard of the "Greatest Show on Earth." But today's press agent for Ringling Brothers and Barnum and Bailey Circus admits in the *New York Herald-Tribune* of March 16, 1960, that he has become "A semi-honest press agent." His name is Joe Shea. While most press agents would say that the circus, which has nineteen elephants, has forty elephants, Joe Shea says it has thirty. Again, he no longer uses "Greatest Show on Earth." He uses when the show is in Boston "Greatest Show in Boston," when it is in New York City "Greatest Show in Manhattan, Queens, Brooklyn, Bronx, Richmond, Nassau, Suffolk and Westchester Counties, including Scarsdale."

Joe Shea's effort to be "semi-honest" in a day of souped-up words is splendid, but why not try to surpass him? Why not try to be honest?

6. *Tricky* words. These are the words that pretend to do one thing but aim to do another or those that aim to do one thing but do another. They are the "hidden persuaders" or hidden dissuaders. The motivational research experts found, according to Vance Packard in his book, *The Hidden Persuaders*, that the term, "low-calorie," which was to have made beer more acceptable made it instead an unpleasant product. For if you drink beer, you want to enjoy it, you don't want to be reminded of the caloric reputation of beer nor do you want to be reminded of diet. You diet to punish yourself for overeating and overdrinking. Who wants to drink a beer that inflicts self-punishment? And so, Blatz came clean with the slogan: "Made by people who like beer for people who like to drink beer—and lots of it."

Suppose you are to speak to a union audience on the proposition, unions must do their part to increase production. Recently the Opinion Research Corporation examined sixty-one of the most common terms in employee communications. It was found that *corporation* to most employees was "big," "selfish," "ruthless," but that *company* was "good," "successful," "necessary." Again, *strike* was a necessary device but *work stoppage* was "bad," "harmful," "unfair." Clearly in trying to win over your union audience you would do well to use *company* instead of *corporation*. You should speak of the policies of the *company*, the financial status of the *company*. And if you scold labor for interference with production, you should use *work stoppage* instead of *strike*. *Work stoppage* has greater emotional impact.

If we are mindful of how words can take us unawares, of how they can stir up unexpected responses, we shall best be able to deal with them in our day to day reading, televiewing, and thinking. If we also keep in mind that advertisers and propagandists are perfecting their techniques in the use of tricky words, we shall be alert.

HOW YOU REASON

Now that you are aware of the three main pitfalls in human thinking —ignorance, bias, and misuse of words—we can discuss how you reason and how you can become more efficient in reasoning. You reason in five different but related ways:

1. From specific instances (Induction)
2. From the general to the specific (Deduction)
3. From analogy or comparison
4. From cause to effect or effect to cause
5. From sign

1. *Reasoning from specific instances* (Induction). The public opinion polls not only gather data but engage in a type of reasoning called "generalization" or "induction." From a sufficient number of people polled and from a sampling which includes a variety of interests, the polls generalize or draw conclusions for the whole population of a state or a section of the country or the nation. Such generalizations are made about many matters; suburbanites who own two cars, women who use Tide soap in Chicago, families watching "Lassie" in California, farmers in Iowa, Illinois, and Indiana who would now vote for President Kennedy.

The public opinion polls have become dependable generalizers. But it has not always been so. A noted magazine, the *Literary Digest,* went on the rocks after the election of 1932 because its survey of the electorate led it to predict that most people would vote for Herbert Hoover. Franklin D. Roosevelt won by a landslide. Since the 1948 debacle of the polls, Gallup and other major pollsters, including those who were not in business in 1948, have refined their techniques to guarantee a valid sample. Thus, to generalize how all the people will vote, they poll a sample which includes in addition to racial and religious factors: occupation, income, home ownership, political party, geographical location, urban or rural area, sex, age, and education. Since 1948, Gallup's election figures have not been off more than 1.7 per cent of the actual results. In 1960, Gallup forecast a 1 per cent margin for Kennedy. "This was the most accurate Presidential poll in our twenty-five years of samplings," said Emery Ruby, executive editor of the Gallup Poll. Other major poll takers—Roper, Kraft, and the Princeton Research Service—were also gratified. "You think we're proud of ourselves," said Kenneth Fink, director of the Princeton poll. "You bet we are!"

But what of our own day to day generalizations? Do you, like most human beings, often commit the fallacy of jumping to a conclusion from a single case or too few cases? Do you read of several juvenile delinquents who are Puerto Ricans, and then generalize that all Puerto Rican juveniles are delinquent? Are you overcharged by a television service man and then conclude that all of them are crooks? Do you get a dozen stale eggs from a supermarket and decide that you will get no more eggs there because they are all stale? Do you have a Plymouth which has given you a lot of trouble and so you resolve never to get another Plymouth because they're all "lemons?" Do you see a Negro in a purple convertible and figure that all Negroes like flashy cars? A teen-ager driving sixty miles an hour passes you on a crowded highway; are all teen-agers, therefore, reckless drivers?

Or suppose you are a man and you are driving along one fine summer morning thinking of this and that and you come to a traffic light which you suddenly see is red. You stop with a screeching of your tires. Someone behind you runs into you. That someone is a woman. From then on will you not believe that women are poor drivers? You will unless you have a larger share of logic than most men.

So, in your thinking and speaking, watch your generalizations. A speaker is not well regarded whose thinking has little connection with fact.

2. *Reasoning from the general to the specific (Deduction).* This type of reasoning is closely related to generalization or induction. You start with the conclusion that you get by generalization. Suppose you have reached the conclusion that all Norwegians are stubborn. You meet a man named Ole Oleson. Very well, Ole Oleson, a Norwegian, must be stubborn. You have applied a general conclusion to a specific person. But it is clear, is it not, that reasoning from all Norwegians to Ole Oleson depends on whether your premise, all Norwegians are stubborn, is sound. The soundness of the premise depends on how fully and fairly you have sampled Norwegians. So deduction, from the general to the specific instance, is completely dependent on induction, which goes from the specific instance to a general conclusion.

You have heard of the syllogism. It is an artificial structure of deductive reasoning. This is the way it looks:

(a) All Norwegians are stubborn.

(b) Ole Oleson is a Norwegian.

(c) Therefore, Ole Oleson is stubborn.

A syllogism is seldom used in ordinary discourse but if you know how it is set up, you can use it to test your deductive reasoning. For instance, what is illogical in the following:

(a) Some Norwegians are stubborn.

(b) Ole Oleson is a Norwegian.

(c) Therefore, Ole Oleson is stubborn.

Is it clear that now you cannot be so sure that Ole is stubborn? For your premise, some Norwegians are stubborn, leaves plenty of room for Ole not to be so. In other words, you cannot reason logically to a specific case unless your premise covers all things or persons. Now if you hear Mr. X say, "Peter Ricaz is a Puerto Rican; watch out for him," you know that Mr. X is illogical because (1) he talks from the premise that all Puerto Ricans are suspicious characters or (2) he talks from the premise that some are. In either case, the deductive reasoning is fallacious, because the premise is faulty.

If we examine our daily thinking, we shall find that we frequently use deduction. And we shall find that if we misjudge a person or an event the error is traceable to a generalization that is faulty, such as, all women are poor drivers.

In Aristotle's day, absolute truth was considered attainable. He formulated the classic syllogism:

(a) All men are mortal.

(b) Socrates is a man.

(c) Therefore, Socrates is mortal.

This syllogism, Aristotle taught, could be adapted to any phenomena. If you were intelligent and educated and zealous in pursuit of the truth, you could reach all-men-are-mortal certainty in all matters. It would be nice if today we could have the certainties upon which Aristotelian logic rested. It would be nice if we could say today:

(a) *All* well-educated people support integration in the schools.

(b) John Jones is a well-educated person.

(c) Therefore, he supports integration in the schools.

Or if we could say:

(a) *All* nations avoid mutually annihilative wars.

(b) Soviet Russia and the United States are nations.

(c) Therefore, they will avoid annihilative wars.

It is the "allness" of Aristotelian logic to which the so-called "new logic" rightly objects. The most we can attain in this complicated world is "someness" or probability. Related to "allness" is the "either—or" dogma:

(a) John Doe is either a conservative or a liberal.
(b) He is not a conservative.
(c) Therefore, he is a liberal.

Today, if we are at all sophisticated, we know that John Doe cannot be so pinned.

Are any of the following either-or premises sound?

(a) Either you are with me or you are against me.
(b) In education you are either a traditionalist or a progressive.
(c) In advertising you are either "creative" or "realistic."
(d) Either he is a criminal or he isn't.
(e) You are either pro labor or con.
(f) Either you succeed in life or you don't.

The trouble with either-or logic is that truth cannot be so patly classified. Take success, for instance. One man's success is another man's failure. One man commits suicide if he cannot maintain his two-Cadillac, Park Avenue-Biscayne Boulevard standard of living; another thinks he has arrived if he makes $10,000 a year. Success is just what you think it is; and everyone has a different idea of it.

3. *Reasoning from analogy or comparison.* Let us suppose that you are debating federal health insurance. Your opponent who is for it argues that a similar system works in England. This is a literal analogy: two actual and related things are under comparison. An analogy can be very effective since it mixes illustration and logic. It needs a clear-cut answer or it may be decisive in an argument.

You could try to dispose of the above analogy by first questioning whether government medicine is, as assumed, a success in England. Your research may have brought out evidence of weakness in that system. If you can make a strong case against it as it is working in England, you destroy the basis of the analogy. But if your opponent produces proof that the English system is successful, then you have two other means of rebuttal. You can point to certain differences between the two plans of government medicine which make comparison invalid. Or you can show how England and the United States cannot be compared with regard to government medicine. There would be such differential factors as: size of population, economic status, experience in state controlled enterprise, adequacy of private medicine in England before the intervention of the government, the great growth of voluntary and industrial group medical plans in the United States, the traditions of the medical professions of the two countries.

Whenever you reason by analogy, the essential test of validity is: Are the things or persons compared really comparable? To reason that continuing inflation will cause a depression in the near future because it caused one in 1929 is to overlook some marked differences: (1) federal insurance of bank deposits today; (2) stricter regulation of speculation in stocks today; (3) an economy today which is geared for the long haul of cold war competition.

There is also the figurative analogy. This is a frequent device of the poet and other imaginative men. It includes the simile and the metaphor. The simile is an express comparison, with *like* or *as:* "Innocent as a dove, cunning as a serpent." The metaphor implies *like* or *as:* He was a Rock of Gibraltar. While figures of speech are useful for graphic effect, they are also part of the reasoning process. A principle or force or action in one set of circumstances is seen to be applicable to another, quite different, set. Obviously operative in one situation, it becomes, through a figure of speech, operative and valid in another. Walter Lippmann once said that we, the American people, are like a man on his way to the West Coast, who, when he gets to Chicago, doesn't know what to do next. The simile sharpens the idea of our confusion; it provides a sound logical jump from a situation that is abstract and generalized to one that is personal and definite.

As with the literal analogy, so with the figurative, you have to be sure that your comparison is sound, that there are fundamental points of likeness.

4. *Reasoning from cause to effect or effect to cause.* You know that the prices are rising. You read that the Consumer Price Index has gone up again. This is an effect of certain causes. The effect you are aware of first; now you look for the causes; you proceed then from a known effect to probable causes.

In an editorial on June 28, 1960, the *New York Times* said of the steadily rising price index:

To the old familiar cause of excessive over-all demand two others have in recent years taken on new importance. The first of these is the autonomous wage push that goes beyond the average rate of increase in productivity; the second is the concentration of demand in one sector, such as, let us say, durable consumer goods, which may be able to increase wages without raising prices. The secondary effect of such concentrated demand may be an increased demand for basic materials such as steel, where costs are high and where a comparable wage increase can be justified, only if accompanied by an increase in prices.

In other words, we have an economic situation in which more than one significant cause operates. The excerpt illustrates the application of two tests of causal reasoning: (1) Is a given cause, "excessive over-all demand," strong enough to produce the effect? (2) Are there other causes —"autonomous wage push" and "concentration of demand in one sector"—that are important?

The excerpt is an example of reasoning from a given effect to probable causes. But you might go instead from a given cause or causes to probable effect. Suppose you decide to eat more to put on weight. The given cause, eat more, should lead to the probable effect, weigh more. This suggests, however, a third test of causal reasoning: Has some factor intervened to prevent the given cause from producing the expected effect? Perhaps you exercise more, or worry more, or sleep less.

So whenever you use or read or hear this most common type of reasoning, the causal, you can evaluate the logic by applying the following tests:

(a) Is a given cause strong enough?

(b) Are other causes at work?

(c) Does something keep a given cause from working?

5. *Reasoning from sign.* This simply means that something is a sign of something else. It is full of possibilities of error. It is the breeding ground of superstition. You walk under a ladder once and five minutes later you are hit by a car; you walk under a ladder again and ten minutes later you fall and break your ankle; you walk under a ladder a third time and that night you fall out of bed and sprain your wrist. So you reason that walking under a ladder is a sign that something bad will happen to you. You do not ask how this can be; you just know that one thing leads to another; no more walking under ladders for you.

Circumstantial evidence is argument from sign. A boy is stabbed. A policeman sees another boy close by who looks nervous. He nabs the boy and searches him. He finds a switch blade, which, together with the boy's nervousness, is a sign that the boy was the stabber. If the boy is innocent, the fact may be hard to prove.

Suppose, if you live in New York City, you see a man on Seventh Avenue neatly attired in a dark, natural shoulder suit with a vest. His tie is conservative, his shoes are shined but unobtrusive, his hat trimly fits his face. Your snap judgment will be that this man is off his avenue, he should be on Madison Avenue, where the well-groomed admen work.

"Some circumstantial evidence," writes Thoreau, "is very strong, as when you find a trout in the milk."

But beware of the argument from sign. It is the pet of the gullible, the impulsive, the suspicious. Paranoiacs thrive on it.

5 THE PEOPLE YOU SPEAK TO

MOTIVES AND INTERESTS

WE NOW ASSUME THAT YOU HAVE SOMETHING TO SAY, that you have gathered data, and that you can use the data accurately and logically. In short, you are a well-informed, thinking person.

But are you going to be able to put across your ideas? The time has come to look at the people to whom you are going to speak. All of us have something in common: human nature. We are all controlled pretty much by the same basic wants: We want health, money, prestige, and love. If you can show us how we can get or keep health, money, prestige, and love, you are "in," you have it made. If you can show us how we can get or keep any *one* of these realities of the good life, you are still "in." If you can show us that the Republican party will cut taxes and also keep us safe from Russia, we'll vote for the party. If you can demonstrate that the United Nations will stave off war, thus protecting us and our loved ones from obliteration, we'll redouble our efforts to support the organization.

The Health Motive

If you can show that your point or proposal is connected with health and longevity, your hearers will be extra-attentive. Self-preservation is an instinct of man and anything that relates thereto is bound to interest him. The overwhelming concern of people today is how to survive in a world threatened by nuclear devastation. If you can show that a proposal or a candidate will minister to our national security and prevent war, you will prevail with any group.

If you are selling cars, do not—in this status conscious world—forget the safety features. Some topics lend themselves more readily to health appeals than others. To argue that the federal government should regulate the prices of drugs has an affinity with health not hard to find. To advertise a toothpaste introduces automatically the health factor. But to contend that the honest preparation of an income tax return is associated with physical well-being may not occur to the advocate.

I do not say that you should find a health and longevity motive in every topic but I do say that you should look for it. Would the following propositions be in any way related to health:

1. Subway fares should be increased to twenty cents.
2. Put aside ten minutes a day for private meditation.
3. The federal government should provide for the compulsory arbitration of labor disputes.
4. Vote for Nixon.
5. Join the Book of the Month Club.

If you find a health motive in every one of the above, you may be stretching a point; but if you consider that whatever contributes to psychological and financial security also has an effect on physical well-being, you can find the motive in just about any proposition. How well you exploit the motive is another matter. You can do it baldly and annoy your hearers; or you can do it subtly, that is, artfully. The artist in speech, as in other activities, is able to conceal his art.

Status—Reputation

Professional and social prestige can be as potent a motivation as health, particularly if one is healthy. Much has been written about the submergence of the individual in a society molded and standardized by mass production, mass media, and corporate pressures. Individual behavior has become, with rare exceptions, predictable. We have organization men. We have status seekers in suburbia and exurbia who aspire "to belong"; they join the "right" churches and clubs, they go to the "right" schools, they live in the "right" towns and in the "right" part of town. Who knows how many Cadillacs are feeding upon modest salaries, so that their owners can feed upon the respect of friends, relatives, colleagues, service station operators, and fellow motorists. Who knows how many people own homes 20 per cent costlier than their incomes allow.

The Schwab, Beatty and Porter advertising agency occasionally has a full-page advertisement in the *New York Times* and other newspapers to illustrate techniques of the trade. In the September 8 and 28, 1960, issues of the *Times*, the agency ran two installments under the heading "100 Good Advertising Headlines." Some of the headlines, which came from many agencies, were new, some old. Note how the following headlines play up prestige or status (reputation, popularity, etc.):

"The Secret of Making People Like You"

"Are You Ever Tongue-Tied at a Party?"
"Who Else Wants a Screen-Star Figure?"
"Do you Make These Mistakes in English?"
"Do *You* Do Any of These Ten Embarrassing Things?"
"Are They Being Promoted Right Over Your Head?"
"Are We a Nation of Lowbrows?"

Explore your topic for a possible tie-in with the prestige motive. Do not strain to use it—that would boomerang. And do not be too obvious about it. If you want to urge people to go to church regularly, you need not say, "Regular church attendance will enhance your prestige in the community." You may not care to use the motive on such a topic, but if you do use it, do it with taste. You might say: "Another advantage of going to church regularly—which, however, is purely incidental—is that you will have a larger role in community activities." Many of your hearers may not regard this advantage as "purely incidental," but they don't mind at all that you put it this way.

Your own apparent status may be a factor in persuasion. Two fire insurance salesmen went before the well-bred schoolboard of a wealthy Massachusetts town to try to sell their policies. Mr. A. was a little lacking in the cultivated manner: his suit had padded shoulders, his grammar was faulty, he was a "hard sell" specimen. Mr. B., however, was "soft sell"; his dress was "right," his accent impeccable. Finally, Mr. B. was a Harvard man, and a Harvard man does not keep his alma mater secret. Which of the two salesmen had better status? Which one got the contract?

Status in this day is a very significant force. The accomplished speaker does not forget it.

Economic Security

Obviously, anything that has to do with our economic security is of irresistible interest. The poor want to get rich and the rich want to get richer. It should not be a cause of great surprise that a long-time occupant of the best-seller list was the book, *How I Made $2,000,000 in the Stock Market*. Almost any topic has an economic implication, although you may not wish to take explicit note of it. For instance, on the reasons for churchgoing you would not make anything of a possible business advantage—or would you? A great deal would depend on whom you were talking to. It would be one thing if you were talking to a few people whom you know well, quite another if you were talking to a larger, unfamiliar group.

Many topics are "naturals" in economic appeal. Anyone speaking to an audience of housewives on "How to Beat Rising Prices" has a cinch; he just needs to be audible. Whoever speaks up for lower taxes can do no wrong—but be careful, there are idealists around who urge higher taxes and more foreign aid because our destiny in the world demands it.

And another thing: Do not try to sell yachts to schoolteachers. Status is important but not at this price.

The Age Factor

The young are more adventurous, or at least they used to be, than the middle-aged or the elderly; they are more ready to undertake a new scheme; they are more idealistic. They have less to lose of the world's possessions, they are not enmeshed in vested interests. In general, the young would be more sympathetic than their elders to such propositions as: capital punishment should be abolished, gambling should be legalized, the tempo of desegregation should be stepped up, the United States should disarm as an example to the world.

In general, the young would need less data to convince them; humor and dramatic illustration would go far with them, as would vigorous gesture and marked vocal emphasis. Understand, we say *in general*. We might be wrong. What is this we hear about the "beat generation" and about the desire of the young to conform? Are they middle-aged before their time? Such questions show that there are no easy formulas governing human behavior.

The Sex of Your Listeners

A woman gave a speech to a mixed audience on "How to Save Money by Doing Your Own Sewing." About half of her listeners were married. The other half were from twenty to twenty-five years old. The speech was a success because the speaker connected her topic with the interests of both men and women, married or unmarried. To the unmarried men, she said something like this: "Now it won't be long before you will be $200 a year richer or poorer depending on whether your wife can sew or not."

Cleveland Amory, prominent observer of American mores and a lecturer much in demand, describes (in the *New York Times Magazine*, January 31, 1960), an audition, a "Spring Preview," of lectures which he attended, and which was sponsored by the country's largest lecture agency for the benefit of the program chairwomen of a number of women's clubs. Each lecturer had ten minutes for his sample. The chairwoman thought a nuclear physicist "very interesting, but he's better for a mixed group." Their reaction to a woman heralded as "one of the finest inspirational speakers on the American platform today" was that "she's very good but so many of our women want their uplift from men." The reaction to another speaker, a foreign correspondent, was ". . . he never talked *down* to us. That's the cardinal sin you know."

Let such reactions guide you when you speak to women. But men, too, have their idiosyncrasies. Beware of jokes on baldness and paunchiness, for instance. Some men take years to get beyond thirty-nine, and no man who finally reaches forty likes to be taken for fifty. Self-respect is a major motivation of men, and many are the slights the poor fellows receive in the workaday world. So the speaker who can make them think better of themselves is bound to get a friendly response. This goes too for you wives with regard to your husbands. A *speaker* is not necessarily a public speaker.

But come back to the women again. Cleveland Amory records another reaction of the clubwomen to a speaker, who was a fashion designer: "Our group is 40's and over. She'd be better for the younger." These clubwomen had candor.

Education and Culture

"Snob appeal" is in vogue these days. The "Sleeping Chamber" in house advertisements replaces the 9 by 14 foot bedroom. "Une maison ranch très originale" replaces an original ranch. But "snob appeal" is not altogether to be lamented. If "snob appeal" can lead some people to buying books or going to concerts or art galleries, that is better than looking at television all the time.

Be careful about "talking down," the "cardinal sin" to the clubwoman. We have gone too far in the "highbrow-middlebrow-lowbrow" classification of people. The ordinary person is cannier than most eggheads realize. He notes and resents condescension. If you talk to an audience of longshoremen and consciously pepper your remarks with profanity and bad grammar, someone as likely as not will cry out, "Can it, Mac!"

We have all encountered the type of person who uses a big word or a foreign one, and then explains it to us. Again, however, we have all heard persons who use technical terms that are not explained but need to be. Sometimes a speaker wastes time and bores his hearers by going over familiar matters. Or, again, he assumes that they know more than they do. But when in doubt about what your listeners know, give them credit for knowing a bit more than they may.

Race and Nationality

Governor Nelson Rockefeller of New York, during the 1960 election preliminaries, went out to North Dakota to test his political appeal. It is a state with a large Scandinavian population. The governor made known that two of his sons were married to Norwegian girls. This was not enough, however, to counteract the Nixon support.

Unhappily, race or nationality too often is the emotional resource of the unscrupulous demagogue. Look at Little Rock. But look, too, at those real estate interests in New York City who spread the report in several neighborhoods that Negroes were coming in.

Adaptation to race or nationality is a legitimate means—if used for decent ends.

Membership in Groups, Churches, Organizations. If you speak to a Lions Club, find out about the objectives and achievements of the organization. Take note of them in your speech. If you support compulsory arbitration of labor disputes, it is one thing if your audience is a union, quite another if it is a chamber of commerce. Would you advocate euthanasia before a church group? Would you support government regulation of drug prices before members of a pharmaceutical association? Maybe you would, but you should know what you are doing. This is not to say that once in a long while the lone, defiant, nonconformist should not have his day. Rather, it is to press home the point that discretion is an attribute of the seasoned speaker. "Innocent as a dove, cunning as a serpent"—a good motto for a speaker.

Occupation and Region

It would be foolish to talk to an audience of dirt farmers on the pleasures of playing tennis. They have enough exercise as it is. Horseshoes, yes, but not tennis. It would be idle to urge before an audience of bankers in a time of tight money that they reduce mortgage interest rates.

It is not only the choice of topic that occupation might determine but also the choice of illustrative material. The accomplished political speaker may have one basic speech, but he varies it as he goes from one region to another to fit occupational interests. The possible defection of farmers in the Midwest makes Republican bigwigs tremble.

A *New York Times* observer of the political campaign of 1960, noting that Nixon depended largely on a single memorized speech, said it "varied from day to day only in variations of its orchestrations." In Sioux Falls, South Dakota, the dominant theme would be how to increase the farmer's income; in Pittsburgh, it would be how to assure steady and profitable employment; in New York City, the emphasis would be on national security. Not that national security was lost sight of at other places, only that the emphasis varied.

It was noted of Lodge, however, that he gave the same speech everywhere with only "a passing swipe" at current news or "a sentence or two" about a local Congressional candidate. But Lodge was a different case; he could afford to dispense with local adaptation. His forte was his services for almost eight years as United States Representative to the United Nations. A vigorous and appealing spokesman, he became through frequent telecasts of United Nations meetings a familiar national figure and in foreign policy a virtual Mr. United States. This special pre-eminence together with the country-wide concern over national security determined the campaign strategy that Lodge should concentrate on foreign affairs. People everywhere were eager to hear him on his specialty.

In September, 1960, Leonard Bernstein, conductor of the New York Philharmonic Orchestra, showed mastery in adaptation to foreign audiences. The orchestra gave two concerts to high school and university students in West Berlin. Bernstein talked on Beethoven, whose music comes "closest of any to the widely held idea of a universal language." In planning his talk, Bernstein had the problem of showing how universality can develop from a "local truth." He decided to use an illustration based on New York's Seventh Avenue, a one-way street. He would show how one-way traffic was the result of New York's congestion, how the congestion was related to the American economy and standard of living, and how domestic and world affairs meshed—thus moving "from local truth about a one-way street to a universal search for truth that is of interest to all mankind."

But when Bernstein got to West Berlin he changed his illustration. He found a condition of much more significance to Berliners than a New York one-way street. Because the airport was in the heart of the city—had to be there because West Berlin, being an island surrounded by communism, had no outskirts—the noise of the airplanes was a besetting problem. Starting with this "local truth," Bernstein spoke of the "kind of rapport that can bring us peace, the immediate and necessary goal of the world."

SELFLESS MOTIVATIONS

Many motivations might arise from your topic and the occasion for a speech, which are relatively selfless, such as: loyalty to country or patriotism, reverence for deity, the pursuit of the good and the true, and concern for peoples of other lands.

The following is an attempt to illustrate how the motivations might figure in a speech:

Are we at a new frontier of morality and character? Do we need a new point of view on self-preservation? It is possible that survival of self and country is in danger if we do not practice our ideals. Democracy is all right, but practice it. Christianity, or any other religion, is all right, but practice it.

The self-seeking pursuit of comfort, pleasure, security, prestige, and wealth will have to give way to an enlightened selfishness. The haves will be have-nots ere long unless men and nations go all out for the general good of everybody everywhere.

It is not sufficient to feel sorry for the downtrodden, shedding tears on our way to the bank. And it is not sufficient to belong to a club that sponsors charity balls but bars "elements" from membership. And it is not sufficient to sit in the house of the Lord on Sunday and put a race in "their place" every day.

6 YOU ORGANIZE YOUR SPEECH

YOU WILL HAVE A MUCH BETTER CHANCE OF SUCCESS IN speaking if you have a clear outline to guide both yourself and your audience. Among the things that vex an audience is a speech in which no points stand out, in which there is no clear-cut progress from one point to another. Such a speech usually has a conclusion that does not conclude, that keeps on going when there is nothing more to say, that seems repeatedly to be about to stop only to get a second wind for another blow at a tired audience.

But the outline is also a boon to the speaker himself. Without one, either on paper or in his mind, he will be less sure of himself, more prone to self confusion. To make a sound outline implies clear thinking. The outline is a test of thinking.

A speech has an introduction, a thesis or statement of aim, a body, and a conclusion.

THE INTRODUCTION

The introduction should arouse interest or establish rapport or put speaker and audience on a common ground. It may accomplish all three objectives; it should certainly accomplish one. Sometimes, but rarely, the best introduction is no introduction at all. An audience of insurance actuaries who are to hear a report on mortality rates is already interested in the subject and needs no preliminaries.

The types of introductions are:
1. Story or anecdote
2. Example
3. Striking first statement
4. Adaptation to local circumstances
5. Adaptation to national and world events
6. Historical background

The story or anecdote, even if told with but moderate skill, arouses interest. The suspense element combined with concreteness captures attention. The humorous anecdote can do much to dispel tensions and antagonisms. It is assumed that the story or ancedote is either germane to the topic or has some pertinence to audience interests or to the occasion.

Following is the introduction to Dr. Banks's speech, "How to Live with Yourself." It is pertinent as well as witty. It arrests attention, puts people in a cordial mood, and is much a part of the subject of the speech.

All behavior has its underlying reason. At the funeral of the richest man in town, a great many mourners turned out to pay their last respects to the dead. Among the multitude was a poor man, who heaved deep sighs. "Are you a close relation of the deceased?" someone asked him commiseratingly. . . . "I'm no relation at all," he replied. . . . "Then why do you weep?" . . . "That's why."

Example, or examples, in an introduction have the primary value of making an idea immediately concrete. Suppose you are to speak on the proposition, Creeping Inflation Is upon Us. You begin like this:

Three years ago you could get Florsheim shoes for $19.95; now you have to pay $23.95. Three years ago you paid $3,250 for your Mercury; today you have to pay $3,750. Three years ago you could have bought a given house for $19,000; today you cannot get it for less than $21,000. Three years ago you could have got Blue Cross-Blue Shield for your family for $85 a year; this year you pay $150.

Such an accumulation of instances not only whets interest but also proves your point. Incidentally, the language illustrates a device that makes for special emphasis. It is antithesis or contrast: in this case, *three years ago* as against *today*. Often it takes the form of *not this . . . but this. . . .*

The striking first statement type of introduction can be a question or questions. It can be an epigram or a proverb or a poetic quotation. It can be a provocative prophecy: "In 1970 the population of the *world* will be only 10 million people. In 1970, New York City, Moscow, London, Paris, Tokyo, and Peiping will not exist." Your topic is: "The Only Solution—Complete Disarmament, Everywhere and Today."

Here is an example of beginning with questions: "Do you know that last month Russia sent two technical missions to the Republic of Ghana to teach agricultural and industrial techniques? Do you know that Russia is training technicians in African languages? Do you know that Russians in Ghana today are four times as many as one year ago?"

The striking first sentence can be in the form of a quotation. " 'I do not agree with what you say,' said Voltaire, 'but I will defend to the death your right to say it.' " Then you go on to your topic, namely, freedom is the right to say what you want to say. Or if you choose to speak against the Welfare state, you might begin with the words of Robert Frost: "I discovered from Bellamy that socialism is everybody looking after Number Two. My criticism was the same then as now: just as conservative. It's harder to look after Number Two than Number One, for how do you know what Number Two wants?"

The type of introduction, adaptation to local circumstances, is effective for establishing common ground and for creating rapport between speaker and audience. Suppose your topic is "We Should Introduce on All Levels of Education the Full Year Session," and your audience is a Rotary Club. In your introduction you could refer to the goals and achievements of the club relating them to your topic: "Your record in the service of the community clearly shows your interest in education. You have sponsored essay and oratory contests. You have contributed to the library. You have set up awards for scholarship. You have supported higher salaries for teachers. You and I are for the best education that human resources can devise. I believe that a full year session is essential to that best education."

In addition to local circumstances, you could refer to happenings in the nation and the world: "Sputnik shook us out of our pleasant dreams of superiority. Sputnik and its successors have forced us to examine our educational systems. Soviet Russia has enthroned science. She has carefully selected and efficiently trained her youth in technology. Russia may win the cold war because she sacrificed comforts and luxuries for hard, intellectual discipline. But it is not too late—yet. It will be soon. I am convinced that one way to hold our own in the cold war is to accelerate the education of our youth. We waste too much time. The long summer vacation is now an anachronism."

You could use separately, or in combination with these introductions, historical background. You could point out that the long summer vacation is a relic of the bucolic past. Years ago the seasonal demands of an agrarian people required that children drop out of school at planting time, not to return until after harvest. That was a long "vacation" indeed! You could say that for a hundred years or more the normal period for elementary and secondary education has been twelve years and that that period grew out of the long March 15 to October 15 "vacation."

The next example, from Charles H. Brower's speech, "The Year of the Rat," mixes two types of introductions, adaptation to current or local circumstances and the use of provocative or striking language.

Those people who believe in statistics tell us that things really boomed in the latter half of 1959. Car loadings were up. Retail sales were up. Dow-Jones averages were up. But the thing that was really up was the production and use of rose-colored glasses. Rose-colored glasses were used in main for gazing happily into the golden haze that came to be known as the Soaring Sixties. Rose-colored glasses are never made in bifocals, for nobody reads the small print in dreams, nor are they interested in handwriting on the wall, or clouds no bigger than a man's hand on the horizon.

There is no arbitrary limit as to the length of an introduction. In general, the longer the speech, the longer the introduction. Some subjects need a great deal of historical background; others need only a statement or two. Some need considerable adaptation to local conditions; others need little. As someone said: "An introduction, like a woman's skirt, should be long enough to cover the subject but short enough to be interesting."

One thing to avoid always in an introduction is apology. The person who apologizes may be well prepared but he is so unsure of himself that he makes people think that he is worse off than he is. An audience takes a speaker at the value he places on himself. If he is apologetic, he hardly inspires confidence.

THE THESIS OR STATEMENT OF AIM

Your thesis or statement of aim depends upon your purpose. Your purpose is to explain, inform, define, or describe; or it is to advocate, convince, or persuade; or it is to impress, please, entertain, or deepen appreciation. Whatever your purpose, you should have it clearly in mind though you need not always explicitly state it.

Once in a while a speaker may decide that the best strategy is to avoid a definite proposition early in his speech. Suppose you were speaking to a local of the United Auto Workers that was agitating for higher wages and was threatening a strike in one week. Suppose your objective was to get the local to postpone the strike for thirty days. Even if we assume that you are a member of the local, you would encounter a hostile audience. It would be better strategy if you withheld a definite proposition until you had presented data about the damaging effects of a premature strike. Of course, your purpose will come through soon anyhow, but your strategy is to let the facts speak for themselves, let the facts lead to a proposition rather than start with a proposition and use the facts to support it.

Again, you do not have to have an explicit proposition for an after-dinner speech. If such a speech amuses or pleases, that is the main thing. That it has or has not a definite thesis stated early or late or not at all is irrelevant. Entertainment is the thing.

If we allow that sometimes the definite thesis should not be stated too early or need not be stated at all, we also stress that in most cases you should have in mind exactly what you are about and should state it exactly.

The following are possible statements of the purposes of the speech to inform, sometimes called the expository speech (assume that you have led off with an introduction, and note that you may state the same thesis in two or three ways—this is not only permissible, it is sometimes essential):

1. "This evening I want to discuss with you the major causes of inflation."

2. "I want to show you how the new Curtiss-Wright engine with only four movable parts works."

3. "I think we should come to a clear understanding of the Forand bill which provides federal medical insurance for the aged."

4. "Nuclear fission—what happens? I want to make this awesome phenomenon clear. I want to show you what happens when a hydrogen bomb explodes."

5. "What does democracy mean? If we can reach agreement on what it mainly means, we should be content. So let us concentrate this evening on the essentials of democracy that all of us can accept."

6. " 'Contemporary house' is a term that seems to cover everything from an early Colonial to an all-glass box. I intend this evening to describe five contemporary houses so that you can grasp more clearly what the term means."

The speech to persuade, also called the speech of advocacy or the speech to convince, embraces sermons and sales talks, jury addresses and political oratory, scientific demonstrations and literary criticism. The objectives are: (1) to convince of the truth of a proposition, (2) to change conduct or a course of action, (3) to sell. The objectives overlap; it is a question of what is stressed.

The following are theses for each objective:

1. To convince of the truth of a proposition
   (a) The conservatism of Senator Barry Goldwater is bedrock Americanism.
   (b) Better dead than Red!
   (c) Society gets the advertising it deserves.
   (d) Can commercial television take care of its own house? No.
   (e) To popularize art is to destroy it—Objection!
   (f) Crime never pays—some of the time.
   (g) A man's worth to society today varies directly with the money he owes.
   (h) A husband should not teach his wife to drive.
2. To change conduct or a course of action
   (a) Communist China should be admitted to membership in the United Nations.
   (b) Support the John Smith bill requiring all owners of houses and buildings to construct fallout shelters.
   (c) Let's rattle some nuclear bombs ourselves.
   (d) Capital punishment should be abolished.
   (e) The farmer should not be paid for non-production.
   (f) If we have bingo, why not slot machines, roulette and "black-jack"?
   (g) Quit worrying: "Sufficient unto the day is the evil thereof."
   (h) "6 Steps to Executive Success."
3. To sell
   (a) Contribute to the campaign of John Doe tonight so that you can have a better city tomorrow.
   (b) You too can afford a Rolls-Royce.
   (c) Subscribe to *Nation's Business,* a "monthly magazine semi-nar."
   (d) Protect your family with the Ironclad program of mortgage—life insurance.
   (e) This portable Tape-O-Phone will increase efficiency and decrease pressure.
   (f) Look good, feel good, and be good—in a Hercules suit.

The theses below are for speeches to impress or stimulate (arouse or deepen appreciation) and for speeches to entertain. While the theses for these speeches may not be explicitly stated, the speaker should have one clearly in mind.

Theses for speeches to impress or stimulate (arouse or deepen appreciation)

1. Albert Schweitzer is one of the grand figures of our time.
2. The paintings of Picasso: fifty years of graphic history.
3. The New Frontier can become reality only with the habits of the old frontier: courage, hard work, and austerity.
4. America will endure—if she deserves to.
5. Dag Hammarskjold lived and died for humanity.
6. Modern commercial architecture: how clean the lines, how functional and efficient.
7. Walking makes for a sound mind in a sound body.
8. "Live alone and like it!"
9. Let me tell you of the marvelous teeming world in a drop of water.
10. The "champs" in any sport are poets of motion.

Theses for speeches to entertain:

1. The tyranny of superlatives: a "colossal" olive is bigger than a "giant" olive.
2. How to be a poor listener: five sure-fire techniques.
3. New York City, the cultural center of the country and a "head-shrinkers'" paradise.
4. Theater, the "fabulous invalid," has survived another year of box office success.
5. I know a lot about modern art but I don't know what I like.
6. Like their parents when they were young, the younger generation is no good.
7. The advantages of being a neurotic.
8. I want to say a few words about my philosophy, Resistentialism, which deals with the resistance of things like the screw driver you can't find or the cap that won't stay on the toothpaste tube.

DEFINING TERMS

There may be terms in your thesis that need definition. You can define by authority, example, word origin, common acceptance, and negation.

The dictionary is, of course, one authority but its definitions are sometimes too general. Whenever possible, refer to specialists. On the meaning of *progressive education*, use educators; on *proportional rep-*

resentation, use political scientists; on *cultural pattern,* sociologists; on *tensile strength,* physicists; on *inflation,* economists.

For the sake of clarity you may need to illustrate the concept. For *progressive education,* use actual school situations, and contrast with examples of traditional education. If the question of a world federation comes up for discussion, it is not sufficient just to quote a specialist on the meaning of federation. Illustrate it with the example of the American federation. Then use the League of Nations, and the United Nations, as contrasting examples.

Sometimes word origin is an effective method of definition. The original meaning of the root of a word may be just the thing for the emphasis of a certain aspect. Take *education,* for instance. It is based on the Latin verb, *educo,* meaning *to lead out of.* Suppose your proposition is: Education should stress the development of creativity. The fact that *education* goes back to *educo* indicates that the English word from its first existence stressed creativity.

The common acceptance of a term can furnish the clearest meaning. To a criminologist, a *criminal* may be a complex being; to a layman, he is one who has been convicted of a serious offense or one who is in a penitentiary. *Truth* or *justice* can be so subtly defined as to escape the understanding of most people who look upon *truth* as fact and *justice* as a square deal.

Negation as a means of definition tells what a term does *not* mean: "Alcoholism does not mean heavy drinking. It does not mean an occasional spree. It does not mean getting drunk. It does not mean two martinis before lunch and three before dinner." Then you say what it does mean: "Alcoholism is the inability to stop drinking once you've taken a first drink."

YOU OUTLINE THE BODY OF YOUR SPEECH

Take the thesis of your speech and break it up into supporting parts. This is an aspect of analytical thinking. When you analyze a topic, you find its main sub-topics. If your analysis is sound, the sub-topics will stand for clearly distinct phases. Suppose you want to explain how a car works. You could analyze the topic as follows:

How a car works:
1. The ignition
2. The carburation
3. The lubrication
4. The cooling system

Here you have four sub-topics. You have met the first requisite of an easy to follow outline. The sub-topics not only support your main topic but they do it in a clear-cut fashion.

Take another example. You are to speak on the topic, what is a contemporary house. Your outline might go as follows:

What is a contemporary house:

1. The Exterior
   (a) Styles
   (b) Materials
2. The Interior
   (a) Walls
   (b) Floors
   (c) Storage
   (d) Kitchens
   (e) Heating

There would be other ways to outline the topic but this one shows that again you have the essentials of a clear approach.

Some topics lend themselves to chronological analysis, that is, division according to time factors. Suppose you are to speak on the evolution of desegregation in this country. Your analysis might be as follows:

Evolution of desegregation in the United States:

1. Civil War period
2. Reconstruction period
3. Adjustment, 1875 to World War I
4. Changes after World War I
5. World War II and changes thereafter
6. 1954 and the historic decision of the U. S. Supreme Court
7. 1954 to the present.

Another kind of topic can best be approached by analyzing it according to causes and effects. Suppose you are to speak on the plight of education in the United States. Here might be your basic outline:

Plight of education in the United States:

1. Effects (what the troubles are)
   (a) Johnny can't read
   (b) Johnny can't write and speak good English
   (c) Russia beats us with Sputnik
   (d) Incompetence of teachers
2. Causes of troubles
   (a) Overemphasis of "permissiveness"

   (b) Overemphasis of "frills"
   (c) The local school boards
   (d) Poor salaries of teachers

So far we have been concerned with the basic outlines of speeches to
inform or explain. Now to specimens of outlines for speeches to persuade. Take the topic, just above, on education. As it stands it is worded
for a speech to explain. But suppose your main objective is to tell your
hearers what to do about the problem. First, you could divide the thesis
into two main parts, (1) the problem, (2) the solution. This is the
problem-solution method, sometimes called the disease-remedy or the
evils-cure method. For the problem part of your outline, you could take
the above cause and effect analysis. The problem would then be divided
as follows:

A. The Problem
   1. Effects
      (a)
      (b)
      (c)
      (d)
   2. Causes
      (a)
      (b)
      (c)
      (d)

Then you add the solution outline, something like this:

B. The Solution
   1. What it is
      (a) Strong state control of education
      (b) Double teachers' salaries within three years
      (c) Programs to develop skills in writing and speaking
      (d) Programs to develop proficiency in the sciences
   2. The Solution is practicable
      (a) Money is available—spend less for third cars, fine liquors,
           and gold-plated faucets.
      (b) Good teachers are available; pay them more.
      (c) Some states exercise strong control over education.
      (d) Some states have already returned to essentials in educa-
           tion.
   3. The solution will remedy the problem (will have great benefits)

(a) It will raise the status of education and educators.

(b) It will increase the number of students who study the sciences.

(c) It will serve notice on Russia and the world that we are on the move.

(d) It will make us into a people that values toughness of mind more than softness of body.

Here is another problem-solution outline:

PROPOSITION: The federal government should institute a program of health insurance for everyone sixty-five years old and over.

(*Problem*) I. There is a need for such a program.

    A. State programs are inadequate.

    B. Voluntary group programs are inadequate.

    C. The aged have lingering, degenerative diseases, which are catastrophic financially.

    D. When the savings of the aged are gone, the burden of catastrophic cost is shifted to relatives or welfare agencies.

(*Solution*) II. A federal program would be practicable.

    A. It could be made a part of the social security system.

    B. The administration of it could be simple and efficient.

    C. The cost of the program would be no greater than the costs of medical care for the aged.

    III. A Federal program would have many advantages over the present system.

    A. It would insure adequate medical care for the aged.

    B. It would eliminate the financial catastrophe of disease for the aged.

    C. It would relieve relatives and welfare agencies of undue financial burden.

You understand that these outlines are just the framework of the speeches based upon them. In actual speaking, you would support each point with one or more kinds of material—specific instances, stories, personal experience, statistics, testimony. In general, depending on the amount of time you have, the more supporting material, the better.

Another type of persuasive speech could not use the problem-solution method of division. Suppose your objective was to convince your audience that Arthur Miller is a greater playwright than Tennessee Williams. First, you would have to determine the criteria by which you can measure merit. Next, you set down positive statements based on the criteria. The following might be your outline:

PROPOSITION: Arthur Miller is a greater playwright than Tennessee Williams.

The criteria:

1. Characterization
2. Language and dialogue
3. Structure or plot
4. View of life

The criteria could them be phrased in argument form, as follows:

1. The plays of Arthur Miller are superior in characterization to those of Tennessee Williams.
   (a) Characters are less extreme
   (b) Character conflicts are more typical of life
   (c) Characters are more varied
2. While the language of Williams is more poetic, that of Miller is more suited to drama.
   (a) That of Miller is efficient and to the point
   (b) That of Miller is more expressive of character
   (c) That of Miller is responsive to a wide range of characters
3. The structure of Miller's plays is tighter, more coherent.
4. Miller's view of life is more accurate than that of Williams.
   (a) Williams overstresses the abnormal and bestial.
   (b) While Miller understands the primitive drives, he also comes to grips with social factors: to Miller man is a social and political being as well as an animal.

If you are preparing a sales talk; the outline would be of the problem-solution type, as follows:

(*Problem*) I. You need a small car for
                (a) Economy
                (b) Maneuverability in heavy traffic
(*Solution*) II. The Volkswagen satisfies your needs.
            III. The Volkswagen has other advantages.
                (a) Comfort
                (b) Safety
                (c) Appearance
                (d) Country-wide repair service

Regardless of the type of speech, after-dinner or welcome or anything else, you will always prepare an outline. Even the impromptu speech, which you have to prepare in a minute or so, should have one. It will not be a thorough outline, you do not have time. But as soon as you get over your surprise at being asked to talk when you did not expect to, or your concern at getting a topic you did not anticipate, you ask yourself: (1) What are the main points of this topic? (2) How should I state the topic? (3) How should I begin? This is not necessarily the sequence of questions to follow but it is the first questions to ask yourself. Answer these questions and a fourth, if possible, What material can I bring to bear on the topic?

Note in the sample outlines on the preceding pages that the points may or may not be in complete sentences. The concern here is with a speaker's outline, one that you use in actual speaking. As such, it should be efficient and easily usable; it should not be like a detailed legal brief —if it were, you would probably bog down in it. A complete brief, for legal or debate uses, serves very valuable purposes: (1) it provides a reader or a judge with all the proofs for a case, (2) it provides its maker with a check of how well the case is proved. But it is usually a bar to direct, conversational speaking; this is particularly true for novices. Many a novice has been instructed to prepare a complete-sentence outline, with every main point and sub-point written out. He gets up to speak, and nine cases out of ten, he will not speak, he will read the outline.

So I insist that you do not prepare a complete-sentence, detailed outline. This does not mean that you do not prepare carefully. But it does mean that you are also prepared for actual speaking; the outline will not get in your way. At most, use occasional complete sentences; specialize in key words and phrases. Then when you speak, you have to extemporize, you will be conversational.

You might, however, write complete sentences for your transitions from one point to another. No transitions, or vague ones, perplex and confuse audiences. Your listeners should know when you are done with one point and when you start another. If you are in doubt that they know, then repeat the point that you have just developed and repeat the point that you take up next. Repetition can be an effective device of emphasis at any time.

There are many ways to make transitions stand out: (1) "first-second-third"; (2) "Our next point is, our last point is"; (3) "Point number two is, point number three is, the fourth and final point is"; (4) "Now that we have considered this argument, let us go to another"; (5) "What is the next issue? It is this, namely . . ."

In actual speaking you might show transition as follows:

1. "We see then that the language of Miller's plays is efficient and to the point. Next we shall see that his language is more expressive of character than that of Williams."
2. "The Volkswagen is not only economical; no other small car can match it in comfort."
3. "Our first point has been that federal health insurance for the aged can be administered efficiently within the social security system; our second point is, while it will provide complete medical care, it will cost no more than medical care for the aged now."
4. "Economy, then, is the first advantage of a Volkswagen. What is the second? It is safety. The Volkswagen is ruggedly built."

In his speech, "How to Live with Yourself," Dr. Banks uses the technique of questions to point up transitions. Early in the speech he says: "I am going to ask you ten questions—ten little questions—that will indicate how well adjusted you may be. Your answers will show whether you know *how to live with yourself.*" The whole of the speech from then on is based on these questions. Each question starts a sub-topic. Each question is numbered and emphasized:

1. *Are you happy?*
2. *Are you ambitious for life?*
3. *Are you socially adjusted?*
4. *Do you have unity and balance?*
5. *Do you give attention to the present?*
6. *Do you have insight into your own conduct?*
7. *Do you have a confidential relationship with someone?*
8. *Do you have a sense of the ridiculous?*
9. *Are you engaged in satisfying work?*
10. *Do you attack your problems promptly and intelligently?*

THE CONCLUSION OF A SPEECH

A conclusion should conclude: it should not be a technique of postponing the end, it should not go on and on and on.

The conclusion can be a summary only. Or it can be a summary interfused with emotional appeals, thus: "We cannot leave Africa to Russia and Communist China. This is a long, cold war for ultimate world domination. We must, as I have pointed out, send to Africa (1) teachers for three-year periods, (2) technical missions for indefinite periods, (3) economic assistance in the forms of surplus food and industrial equipment. Let us not forget that Red China and Russia are penetrating everywhere in Africa. Africa wants us, Africa needs us, and we need Africa."

If the speech is short, no summary may be needed. If the speech is long, so that one is needed, do not let the summary get too detailed. Stick to main points.

You can conclude with pithy or provocative statements: "When God contemplates this little globe, does he say, 'Better two Cadillacs in an American's garage than a square meal in an African's hovel.'" You might have a series of challenging rhetorical questions: "Shall we go on depriving many of our aged of adequate material care? Shall we continue to plague the aged with catastrophic costs? Are we willing to admit that the ills of the aged are no concern of government? Shall we let vested interests triumph over the sick and the needy?"

You can conclude with a story or a graphic illustration.

If you have made an action speech, end by showing what specifically your hearers can do. Make the action simple, easy, and definite. Show the *how*, the *where*, and the *when*.

However you choose to conclude, end on a decisive note. Watch out for the after-thought: "Oh, yes, I forgot one thing . . ." And watch out for a lame or apologetic ending. Heed the advice: "Stand up, speak up, and shut up."

7   YOU PHRASE YOUR IDEAS

NEVER UNDERESTIMATE THE POWER OF THE WORD—BOTH the right word and the wrong one. It may well be that the biggest single factor in winning, or losing, arguments, or in arousing a favorable or an unfavorable audience response is language. The adept in language can clarify, or if he wishes, cloud meaning; he can be quite correct or he can indulge in slang and solecisms; he can be graphic, provocative, diplomatic. He has an accurate, sensitive vocabulary. He knows how to arrange words for best effect. The great preachers and the famous lawyers are all masters of language.

Earlier, I discussed words as bars or aids to clear thinking. Here I discuss them as ways of making your ideas effective.

1. *Work for accuracy*. There are differences of smallness, swiftness, funniness; differences in walking, jumping, talking; differences in any area of meaning. In choosing words, try to get close to the exact shade of meaning—*make this a habit*. An object can be *microscopic, minute, tiny, undersized, dwarfish, stunted*, etc. A person can be *fast, nimble, agile, speedy, fleet, mercurial, electric*. Someone can be *witty, humorous, jolly, jovial, jocund, amusing, droll, sportive*. In jumping, you can *leap, vault, spring, bounce, bound, hop*. In talking, you can *utter, pronounce, orate, declaim, spout, rant, ramble, lecture, woolgather*. A person attentive to the wishes of others can be *responsive, receptive, suggestible, susceptible, sensitive, pliable, ductile, malleable, resilient, spineless*. Someone who toys with the truth *misleads* or *misrepresents* or *distorts* or *exaggerates* or *overdraws* or *lies* or *prevaricates* or *deceives*.

These few of the possible synonyms for a word are a fair indication of the possibilities for exactness. A synonym is not a perfect substitute for another word; it is similar in meaning but enough different to be exactly the word for your purpose.

2. *Work for clarity*. Your words may be accurate but they may be unclear, too. You might want to use *miniscule* for extreme smallness, but some in your audience might not know the word; use *minute* or *tiny*. While *inimical* may be the closest word to a shade of meaning, *hostile*

or *antagonistic* or *unfriendly* is clearer. It depends on the particular audience. Technical words may be accurate and clear to specialists in a field but unclear to laymen. *Over-assimilation* makes clear sense to speech teachers, but *slovenly pronunciation*—"whadja say"—makes more sense to their students. *Parturition* is fine for obstetricians, but *childbirth* is better for their patients. *Caries* is excellent for dentists, but *decay* means more to their clients. If there is any question about the clarity of a term, always explain it. If you are speaking on *legalized gambling*, make the term clear: Tell what it does and does not cover, illustrate it. The same goes for *juvenile delinquency, desegregation, health insurance, educational television.*

On the other hand, let us face it, there are times when clarity is not what you want. If you are an editor and you find a manuscript badly written, your letter of rejection may say: "While your manuscript has undoubted merits, we think that it does not meet the needs of our list at the present time." If you are at a committee meeting and you are against a proposed plan you might say: "Though I see certain benefits of the plan, I feel very strongly that we should wait until all the facts are in." The strategy of ambiguity is, whether we like it or not, in common use, from the United Nations to the backyard fence. It is as common among the empire builders in the halls of higher learning as it is among the denizens of the halls of Congress who eyeing the next election do not want to be understood too clearly back home.

In short, be clear, be very clear, when you want to be.

3. *Use correct language.* I am not fastidious or "pure" as to grammar. I would not object if you said, "I will go," to express simple intention of going, instead of, "I shall go," or if you said, "If he was present," to express what is contrary to fact, instead of "If he were present." Nor would I object if over the telephone you answered when I called, "It's me." Again, if you said, "Those kind of apples" instead of "That kind of apples," I would not be disturbed. Even if you said, "Does everyone have their coat?" instead of "his coat," I would be calm. Dangling prepositions are not anathema to me nor are split infinitives: "What do you want it *for*?" or "What are you interested *in*?" is quite acceptable, as is "I want *to emphatically declare*" or "He tried *to abruptly stop* the talk."

Also, slang is acceptable if you don't overdo it. Even Trumanesque profanity, if it is not a regular feature of language and if it is right for the occasion, is not a rhetorical sin. Though Republicans condemned it,

Truman's language at a $50-a-plate Democratic dinner in San Antonio, Texas, October 10, 1960, was, if patently robust, suitable to the occasion: "The damn farmers vote Republican. They ought to have their heads examined. . . . Nixon is against labor—against public housing—against public power. He is against public health funds. I don't know what the hell he's for. . . . And that bird has the nerve to come to Texas and ask you to vote for him."

Emancipation from puritanism in language does not, however, mean licentious wallowing in error. I am for direct, accurate, clear language. Because an error becomes popular, it does not become correct. I refuse to believe, despite the new *Webster's International Dictionary*, that *ain't* is now in good odor. What comes natural is not correct until what is correct comes natural. The distinction which I make between good usage and bad, a distinction that will satisfy nobody, is not so much between correct and incorrect as between what is direct, accurate, clear, and cultivated and what is artificial and pedantic.

What does *cultivated* mean? You would give me a turn if you said, "You was there" or "We was surprised" or "Neither he nor I are going." I would be upset if you said, "I laid down and slept" or "I set down and ate," or "I seen," "He done it," "I have went."

Other errors I would rather not hear are:

I brung it home.
I drunk it up.
He has forgot it.
He was hung at dawn.
He rung the bell.
Neither of the salesmen have come.
Each of them have a job.
You will hear from John and I.
He sat besides me.
The data was gathered last week.
Between you and I, he's a liar.
It was broke yesterday.
No one came but him and I.

The best practical criterion of usage, one that allows for evolving changes and occasional liberties but still implies high standards, is—how do most well-educated people express themselves.

4. *Use a variety of words.* Avoid the overuse of such easy adjectives as *big, great, nice, pretty, good, wonderful.* Diversify your active vocab-

ulary, the vocabulary you use in speaking and writing, by practicing with synonyms for overused words. If you use *show* too much, practice with *prove, demonstrate, uphold, confirm, bolster, substantiate, reinforce, evidence, portray, delineate.* Use a word five times and it goes from your passive to your active vocabulary; *passive* is your vocabulary of recognition, it contains the words you know when you hear or read them but do not actually use. An enthusiastic student of speech made it a point to use words daily that he had not used before; he practiced them in sentences as he walked to and from his office, 45 to 60 minutes a day. He soon developed a wide and efficient working vocabulary.

Watch out for clichés: strong as an ox, surly as a bear, quick as a flash, drunk as a lord, sober as a judge, smooth as silk, sly as a fox; he ran like a deer, he swam like a fish, he cried like a baby, he roared like a lion, he ate like a pig.

Watch out for such hackneyed expressions as:

method in his madness	no sooner said than done
beauty is as beauty does	better safe than never
the better half	along these lines
the fairer sex	through thick and thin
in the arms of Morpheus	by the sweat of one's brow
without rhyme or reason	out of the frying pan into the fire
to all intents and purposes	snare and delusion
the wish is father to the thought	the long and the short of it
his bark is worse than his bite	conspicuous by his absence

5. *Use a variety of sentences.* Short sentences should prevail in a speech, but this does not mean that most sentences should have no more than five words. It does mean that too many sentences like the following would confuse and irritate your hearers:

The major causes of inflation—and by inflation I mean high prices going higher—are the escalator clauses in union contracts, which means that wages automatically go up when prices go up, the increase in demand for goods, and services including everything from more steaks to luxurious reducing salons, two Cadillacs, and a mink coat for Fido, and the continuance of a cold war, that might become hot, economy.

As Shakespeare says, the end of the sentence has forgot its beginning.

Note in the following excerpt from Dr. Murray Banks's speech the short, varied, and emphatic sentences. Note that:

1. Questions are often used, as in the whole speech.

2. Imperative sentences—sentences of mild to strong command—are used.
3. Sentences often begin with *you*. Pronouns like *you, your, I* abound.
4. No sentence is too long.
5. No one type of sentence is overused.
6. The whole effect is one of energetic directness.

I am going to ask you ten questions—ten little questions—that will indicate how well-adjusted you may be. Your answers will show whether you know how to live with yourself.

1. Are you happy? "Happy? I'm miserable, just miserable."

Such an answer indicates that you have a high "personality fever" and are not making the most effective adjustments to everyday problems. Happiness comes as a by-product to effective striving for desirable goals. It is never something you can get directly.

Don't confuse happiness and pleasure. Pleasure you can buy. You can buy an evening in a nightclub or a theater. You can buy a week in the country. But you can't buy happiness.

If your life has purpose, if you set up desirable goals and work to attain these goals then happiness comes to you. It comes to you as a by-product— your reward for good living.

2. Are you ambitious in life? At any age, from two to ninety-two, are you interested in life, in love, in work, in play? Have you zest for living? Be ambitious for life, but not beyond your ability. A parent should not attempt to fit a square peg in a round hole. Only tragedy can result when one attempts to make an engineer out of a moron.

Questions stimulate; they reach out and grab attention. Imperative sentences like, "Don't confuse happiness and pleasure" and "Be ambitious for life, but not beyond your ability" put the matter squarely up to you; you can avoid the impact of a sentence like "One ought to be ambitious for life" but not of a sentence that begins with "Be ambitious" for it nails *you*. Advertisements abound in orders like "Change to," "Try today," "Mail coupon now," "Drive-in for Coke."

So at times get away from the polite distance of the impersonal declarative sentence. Make your hearers wake up and think with questions. Shoot commands at them. Startle them now and then with exclamations, such as:

1. "The cigarette, what a tyrant! So thin, so tiny, but what a tyrant!"
2. "Castro, the champ of long distance running at the mouth!"

3. "No United Nations! What a nightmare!"

4. "What nonsense! What drivel! That the aged do not want federal health insurance! How wrong can a survey be!"

Now and then, for emphasis, you might use such language devices as parallelism, antithesis, and direct discourse. Parallelism is the repetition of sentence structure, as in this excerpt from one of Winston Churchill's great war speeches: "We shall fight on the beaches, we shall fight on the landing grounds, we shall fight in the field and in the streets, we shall fight in the hills; we shall never surrender."

Still another instance from President Roosevelt's radio speech to the American people the evening of December 9, 1941:

In 1931, ten years ago, Japan invaded Manchukuo—without warning.

In 1935, Italy invaded Ethiopia—without warning.

In 1938, Germany invaded Czechoslovakia—without warning.

In 1939, Germany invaded Poland—without warning.

In 1940, Germany invaded Norway, Denmark, The Netherlands—without warning. . . .

The parallel structure continues for five more sentences. The power of the device, given an occasion of great import and urgency, is irresistible.

Antithesis is a technique of sentence structure that stresses contrast. An example:

With a policy of systematic technological and economic assistance to emergent Africa, we shall attract her to democracy, not force her to communism; we shall see healthy, enterprising peoples, not starving, disease-ridden, shiftless mendicants; we shall be equal to our responsibilities and destiny, not subservient to indifference and selfishness; we shall exemplify high national moral purpose, not the dominance of "dollar diplomacy."

Direct discourse or dialogue produces an animated, dramatic illustration. The potency of Dr. Banks's speech is in part attributable to his liberal use of direct discourse, for example:

On the other hand I remember a man who sat in my office one day and, on the way out sighed, "You know, Doctor Banks, I wish I had gone to college."

"Well, why don't you go?" I asked.

"Because I'm thirty-five years old, married, have two children, and it would take me ten years to go to college at night."

"Tell me," I asked, "how old will you be in ten years if you go."

"Why, I'll be forty-five years old!" he exclaimed.

"And how old will you be in ten years if you don't go?"

He thought a moment and said slowly, "Uh, forty-five, I guess," and was completely confused that the age came out the same.

Next time you say to yourself, "Oh, I can't do that. I'm too old," ask yourself: "How old will I be if I don't do it?" And if you get a younger answer, please write or phone me immediately!

6. *Use lively, graphic, vivid words.* I would add to the saying, "It is the business of an orator to change the ears of an audience into eyes" the words: "and also to make the ears hear, the mouth taste, the nose smell, and the skin feel." In other words, the effective speaker, like the effective advertiser, should use words that stimulate all the senses.

In the realm of the sense of taste we can speak of a person as sweet, sour, vinegarish, acid, tart, bitter, or bland. We can say that a statement is salty or peppery.

The sense of smell, as Roy Bedichek points out in *The Sense of Smell,* is "the inarticulate sense." There are few words that are peculiar to odors. We have *red, blue, yellow* for colors but no equivalent for odors. If we say that an odor is *penetrating* or *piercing,* we borrow words from the tactile sense, the sense of touch. If we say that it is *fragrant* or *aromatic,* we use a general, not a specific, term. And if we say it is *musky,* or *moldy,* we use metaphor: we compare it to the odor of musk or mold. But it matters little that the sense of smell is without its own words. If we can stimulate it, that's all that matters.

The tactile sense, the sense of touch, is responsive to stimuli of pain, pressure, temperature, and texture. A *hot* idea or a *hot* issue or *hot* news or a *hot* war; or *soft* sell and *hard* sell; or a *coarse* or a *prickly* or an *oily* person; or a *searing* experience; or a *caustic* manner; or a *sultry* voice; or he *sweated it out;* or she *froze* at the sight of him; or the proposition left me *cold*—these expressions, some in common use, show how an idea or an impression can be given tactile concreteness.

Then there are the many words that utilize the kinesthetic sense, the sense of bodily movement and tension. You can energize your thoughts with expressions like the following:

He *leaped* into the argument.

He *jumped* at the opportunity.

Tread softly or you will *stir up* the cats.

How he *crawled* before the opposition.

Her eyes *danced* with excitement.

Unpaid taxes and interest *crushed* him.

He is the *pushy* type.

Not to support farm prices at 100 per cent of parity is to *throttle* the farmer.

To go on with capital punishment is to *whip* the public conscience. *Hit* him with that argument and *hit* him *hard.*

The above kinesthetic words are metaphors. You apply the physical sense of the word to a psychological or mental state. You make a comparison without the use of *like* or *as.*

The simile is an explicit *like* or *as* comparison. Like the metaphor it adds appeal, force, or cutting edge to meaning:

To yield to the farmer's demands for price supports at 100 per cent of parity would be like increasing your children's allowances whenever they asked for it.

A three-man secretariat at the United Nations would be as sensible as a three-man presidency of the United States.

As the steady inflating of a balloon will "bust" it so the steady rise of prices will "bust" our economy.

There Khrushchev sat, pounding his fists like an overgrown brat.

The Castro regime is like state beatnikism.

Architecture is like frozen music.

Another device that has vividness is synecdoche: the part standing for the whole, thus:

"Dollar diplomacy."

Let nations forswear the sword for the word.

He is a devotee of the bottle.

"Lend me your ears."

Let us break bread together.

The full mind is a surer way to happiness than the full pocketbook.

7. *Use epigrammatic language.* An epigram or proverb or pithy phrase puts an idea or impression in decisive language. It steps up the power of an idea. If your hearers forget everything else you say, most of them will remember the epigrammatic bits. This does not mean that most sentences should be sententious gems; too much of a good thing dulls the goodness. A gem now and then is sufficient. Note how the following statements arrest attention and stimulate thought:

"Every reform was once a private opinion." Emerson.

"When it comes to doing for others, some people stop at nothing." General Features Corporation quoted in *Reader's Digest,* July, 1960.

"Vote for the man who promises least; he'll be the least disappoint-

ing." Bernard Baruch, in *Meyer Berger's New York* by Meyer Berger.
"Equality of opportunity is an equal opportunity to prove unequal
talents." Viscount Samuel, *Reader's Digest,* September, 1960.

"Middle age is when your narrow waist and broad mind begin to
change places." Ben Klitzner, *Reader's Digest,* July, 1960.

"Writing free verse is like playing tennis without a net." Robert Frost,
Time, July 4, 1960.

"What adds to the confusion in this space age is that prophecy gets to
be history before it becomes current news." Herbert Bayard Swope,
Jr., *Reader's Digest,* September, 1960.

8. *Use tactful language.* Do not forget Mrs. Clare Boothe Luce who, in
1959, had to give up the ambassadorship to Brazil as a result of her
news release about Senator Wayne Morse: "My difficulties of course go
some years back and began when Senator Wayne Morse was kicked in
the head by a horse." And do not forget Secretary of Defense Wilson
who likened unemployed men who looked to the government for jobs to
kennel-fed dogs who "sit on (their) fanny and yell." What an outcry
from unions and politicians!

In his book, *How I Turned $1,000 into a Million in Real Estate,* Wil-
liam Nickerson advises the use of *owner* instead of *landlord:* "The New
Deal fostered a bitter reaction to 'Landlord.'" He also advises the
avoidance of *janitor;* use *manager.* And if you want to employ a "higher
class manager," refer to "the dirty work as 'maintenance' or 'custodial.'"
So don't ask a manager, "Are you the janitor?"

An instructor in reading, Dr. Frank C. Laubach, reports that in trying
to recruit illiterate students at a factory in Charlotte, North Carolina,
for a reading course over television he was able to sign up only three
with an approach keyed to the question, "Would you like to read?" But
when he changed to "Would you like to learn to improve your reading?", he attracted fifteen. The point? Talk up to your hearers, not
down to them.

Do not say to a person that he is *wrong,* he is only *mistaken;* or that
he is *stupid,* he is only *misguided* or *misled* or *misinformed;* or that he's
incompetent, he's only *unsuited* to the job. Do not tell someone, "You
do not deserve a promotion" when you can say, "The time for your
promotion is not far off." And don't call someone to his face a *reac-
tionary* or a *bigot* or a *liar.* Avoid name-calling altogether, unless of
course the names are complimentary or unless you have a definite purpose in mind. I have said that invective, which includes the art of name-

calling, is a staple of British political rhetoric. The purpose, to undermine or cut down an opponent to size, is considered legitimate.

The matter of tactful language points again to that prime criterion of skill in speaking, the ability to do or say whatever suits a particular situation.

8 YOUR WAY OF SPEAKING

EMERSON WROTE, "WHAT YOU ARE STANDS OVER YOU THE while, and thunders so that I cannot hear what you say to the contrary." This puts well the prime importance of personality in speech. There are some people you just naturally like, some you distrust, some you have confidence in, and some about whom you could not care less. The impression created too often by Thomas E. Dewey during his campaign speeches in 1948 was of a man slightly smug and stilted. He had a fine, resonant voice and he used it well; he had excellent stage presence and effective bodily action; he had great debating skill. But he did not have the elusive plus factor; call it "oomph" or political sex appeal. Another way of putting it is that he did not have built-in friendliness. In 1948 he was up against a less cultivated speaker; he offered an excellent voice against one only adequate; correct language, against everyday usage. But Dewey was also up against a man who echoed the hearts of most of the people. He was up against a man who on his famous whistle-stop tours liked to say from the platform of his railroad car, "Now let me introduce you to the boss," and out would come Mrs. Truman, and then say, "And now let me introduce you to the boss of the boss," and out would come daughter Margaret. Harry Truman pulled no punches, he talked like anyone else, he made it known that he didn't like anyone who criticized his daughter and that he would punch even a music critic in the face. In short he was plain Harry Truman, American, and the whistle-stop audiences loved it.

I have already commented on the television images of Richard M. Nixon and John F. Kennedy in the election of 1960. Now a word about the case of Senator Hubert Humphrey of Minnesota, as fine a speaker as there is in public life. He got nowhere in the primaries against Kennedy. What was the trouble? Many people felt that Hubert Humphrey could talk too well about too many things and that perhaps words took the place of action. Maybe he was trying to pull the wool over somebody's eyes.

This is not to say that Hubert Humphrey, or Thomas Dewey, lacked appeal as speakers. After all, both did attract many voters. Both were effective, if not so effective as their rivals. The point to be stressed is that personality may be the decisive factor.

PERSONALITY TACTICS IN SPEAKING

Tactics of personality! Before you dismiss this as hypocritical, consider how much of our time and our thought each day is given over to what to say and how to say it? Do you always tell people exactly what you think of them? Do you always give the real reason for doing something? Do you tell "white lies?" Are we not all strategists in our day-to-day living?

Aristotle in his treatment of rhetoric, which is the art of persuasion, discusses the concept of ethical proof. Such proof comes from the character, intelligence, and personality of a speaker. It has to do with the speaker himself as a person, apart from the material he presents. You may have a great deal of data on a matter and yet get nowhere because you are a "sourpuss." Or you may have skimpy data and yet carry the day because of the way you smile. If you seem to be kind, modest, honest, genial, straightforward and intelligent *while you are speaking,* you will be irresistible. But it is *while you are speaking* that counts. Off the platform you may be a liar or a crook or a monster, but on the platform, if you seem to be a Dr. Jekyll and your audience knows nothing of Mr. Hyde, you will be applauded. Your ethical proof will be strong. Ethical proof, then, is the persuasive force of what you are or *seem to be* while you are speaking.

Now to the traits and tactics of personality:

1. *Sincerity.* A lot of nonsense has been vented on the catchword, "Be Yourself." It is not enough to be yourself in order to drive a car; you should know how to drive. It is not enough to be yourself to remove someone's appendix; preferably you should have had training. Be yourself, yes, but be yourself *trained.* St. Augustine said: "Love the Lord thy God with all thy heart, and then do as you please." So be yourself, or do as you please, when you are something other than an untaught primitive.

The same goes for those chants that lead to mediocrity, "Be Sincere," "Be Natural." Sincerity is a virtue but not by itself. Sincerity plus knowledge, experience, and technique—yes.

There are brands of tactical sincerity. Consider the "boyish" man. He is always chipper. He laughs a lot and capers about. But make no mistake about it: he knows where he is going and he gets there.

Then there is the bluff, hearty man given to outbursts of frankness.

He may be what he seems to be; or he may be what Mark Antony really was, cunning and devious and artful, he who said of Caesar: "I am no orator, as Brutus is; but, as you know me all, a plain blunt man." Plain and blunt indeed! But for the reading of Caesar's will, this "plain blunt man" tactic was the final incitement to riot.

2. *Liveliness.* To be lively does not mean that you act like the evangelist, Billy Sunday, who was never so much in his element as when he was jumping up and down in the pulpit or throwing chairs around.

I recall a speaker who used to antagonize everybody, even those who agreed with him. He tore passions to tatters. Calm down, I said, at least now and then. If you stress everything, you stress nothing.

A more frequent fault is apathy. Since nothing seems to happen in the speaker, nothing happens in the audience—except boredom.

Two noted lecturers come to mind, whose styles of speaking are poles apart: Robert Frost, the poet, and John Mason Brown, the drama critic. Frost speaks slowly most of the time, has long pauses, seldom has marked changes in pitch or force. Yet the throb of life is felt. The intensity of sense and insights is felt. John Mason Brown has a more obvious liveliness. Call it histrionic. His manner and his vivid language are kin. At times he races; at times he effervesces.

Both Frost and Brown are highly effective. Liveliness is a personal intensity of thought and speech.

3. *Tact.* One of the most useful traits for a speaker, tact, implies a knowledge of people. It means deftness in dealing with them. It expresses itself in many ways. It is a guardian of the words you use. You will not say, "Now do you get this through your head," instead of "Have I made this clear?" You will not say your wife is forty, when she is forty. May it not be said of you that you have the "foot-in-mouth disease."

The tactful speaker is no "loudmouth." Nor is he a know-it-all. He is without condescension. Having a basic respect for the other fellow, he is modest, friendly, and courteous.

There are times when anger and bluntness are in order or when sarcasm and invective are relevant. But such occasions are few.

Even at a time of unusual stress when, let us say, you debate with a vehement opponent, and before an audience intensely partisan pro and con, such an issue as, Should Communist China Be Admitted to the United Nations—even then you might find that a soft answer gets you farther than a bitter word.

4. *Poise.* A wide-reaching concept, poise covers your philosophy of

life, temperament, the state of your pocketbook, your successes and failures, your experience and know-how as a speaker. The poised speaker is one who has things under control; he knows the arts of speech and can apply them with acumen; he can do what a situation calls for. If it calls for humor, he can supply it; if it calls for solemnity, he has it. If a word or a phrase needs emphasis, he knows what to do and how to do it.

The poised speaker does not expect to be perfect; he expects to slip up now and then and is not "thrown" when he does; he knows that nobody is so good that he is not at times less than good.

The poised speaker does not expect the rapt attention of everybody. He would be amazed if he got it.

Suppose you are talking to a committee. How would you act if the chairman, for instance, looked out the window most of the time or if he repeatedly yawned? Or if a member bowed his head and closed his eyes as if in sleep or if he cast pregnant looks at other members when he was not looking at the ceiling or if a member fiddled with his watch, even shaking it once or twice? Some people would like nothing better than for you to be upset by their antics. Know this and foil them.

Consider another situation. Suppose you have been at odds with someone who is now among your listeners. You notice as you speak that he is talking to his neighbor and laughing. This may nettle you, but you should not let it get you.

The poised speaker is truly the philosophical man. In the context of the pressures and perversities of the human world he comes close to attaining what the professional philosophers seldom attain: a realistic mastery of self.

BUT WHAT SHALL I DO WITH MY HANDS

Put your hands where they are comfortable. If you want to put them behind your back, do so. If you want to fold them over each other in front, do so. If you want to put them in your pockets, do so, but—don't keep them there all the time. The essential point about your hands, your gestures, your posture, and your facial expression is that they aid you. If a gesture or other movement calls attention to itself, it needs to be changed or eliminated. If lack of gesture weakens what you say, something ought to be done about it. The only practical test of bodily action is what it does to your message.

A woman gave excellent speeches, but at first she had the habit of holding her chin too high. This made her seem uppity, supercilious, and

it annoyed many of her listeners. Yet she was not what she seemed. Here
was a little thing in itself, but it called attention to itself. She was made
aware of it and she held her chin down. A man was a good speaker except for a mannerism of gesture. He used only one kind of gesture. With
index finger pointed, he briskly sawed the air with an up and down,
across the body, arm movement. His audience would notice the gesture,
then would be mesmerized or repelled by the monotony of it. They lost
what he said. Soon, however, he developed other gestures and used his
pet one but little.

1. *Types of Gestures.* We shall describe the types of gestures so that
you may practice them, not because you need to use them all in a single
speech; some might not be appropriate either to meaning or to yourself
or to the occasion of your speech. It is silly to raise your hands above
your head in wide, sweeping, emotional gestures if you are presenting
mortality data to an audience of actuaries. Again, since we are not
all similarly constituted either physically or temperamentally, to say
that everybody should be able to use all types of gestures would be
to defy the Creator. There are quiet folk and exuberant folk, there are
the fat and there are the lean, there are those who would rather wear a
hair shirt than disport themselves on the platform and there are the born
hams who would rather wear a hair shirt than not disport themselves.

Still you can and should practice all these basic types of gestures. For
only by practicing all of them do you discover those you can use best.

(a) *Index finger,* the pointing finger. Sometimes this gesture scolds
   or it denounces; it always singles out a point for sharp emphasis.

(b) *Palm* or *palms up.* This gesture asks for rational deliberation or
   it appeals for acceptance of a point of view. It says, "Come, let
   us reason together," or "Is not this the best course of action to
   follow?" The palm or palms up and the arm or arms stretched
   outward and upward above the plane of the head express inspiration, exaltation, or great reverence.

(c) *Palm* or *palms down.* This gesture pacifies or pronounces a bless-
   ing. Sometimes, on a low plane with a brisk repetitive sidewise
   action, it indicates a violation of rules or quick, decisive rejection.

(d) *Palm* or *palms out.* The gesture pushes away, expresses aversion
   or disgust.

(e) *Hand* or *hands vertical.* The hand, like a meat cleaver, cuts up
   and down. It is a gesture that explains and analyzes.

(f) The *fist.* Obviously this gesture provides aggressive emphasis.
   But fisticuffs are not included.

In addition to these basic gestures there is an infinity of personal and descriptive gesture. Think of those dexterous makers of pizza pies who stretch out on their arms and hands the thin round of dough, slap it about, and toss it up and down. You may know an effervescent person; think of the ceaseless physical activity: the grimacing, the hands now flung out in despair or upward in ecstasy, the fingers twisting and turning frenetically.

Try out the basic gestures. Experiment. Practice. Do not be concerned about too much action. Few people have that fault. Most people have too little action. Many feel self-conscious when they gesture; some have the curious notion that gestures are undignified or unsophisticated. Nonsense!

When we say *practice*, we mean practice with sentences and groups of sentences. Practice a speech, using copious and varied gesture.

While gestures are useful for emphasis, there are two incidental values that apply to bodily action: (1) the purge, and (2) the mnemonic. One of the best ways to purge the soul—the word *soul* is making a comeback —of excess tension is physical activity. This applies to gestures as well as to playing tennis, taking a long, fast walk, or battering a boxing dummy. If you gesticulate freely while speaking, you will quickly lose your self-consciousness or sense of awkwardness. If you have stage fright, bodily action will ease it.

The mnemonic effect of bodily action is based on the intimate association of all the stimuli and responses in a stimulus-response pattern. A gesture or movement can jog the memory. This is especially true if you have practiced your speech with gesture and movement. When you are actually presenting the speech, you may momentarily forget what to say next. If you take a step or two or lift your hand to gesture, this may be enough to bring the forgotten thing to mind. The gestures and movements of your practice are part of the pattern of your ideas and words. A gesture or movement can activate an idea or word just as a string around your thumb can remind you to bring home meat for dinner. The reverse is also true: an idea or a word can evoke the gesture that you used in practice.

2. *Essentials of Any Effective Gesture.* Gestures to be effective have to meet the following minimum essentials:
   (a) They must not rivet attention on themselves.
   (b) There should be a variety. No one gesture should be overused.
   (c) There should be adaptation to meaning and feeling. Do not use a fist gesture for a trivial point. Do not use a fist gesture if you are

asking for cooperation; if you are demanding it, that is another matter. Obviously you would not use the palm out gesture to indicate agreement or acceptance. Neither would you use the index finger to express emotional bliss.

(d) Gestures should be well timed. A gesture is at its best when its fullest physical impact is exactly coordinated with the word or words to be stressed.

(e) Avoid excessive gesture. Not many people have this trouble. But those who do should remember the chief purpose of gesture—emphasis. To gesture all the time emphasizes nothing.

(f) Gestures should fit the audience and the occasion. The larger the audience, the larger and more vigorous your gestures; this also applies to the younger audience. Certain occasions call for little gesture. Presenting a financial report to a group of bankers might not require any gestures; the figures themselves speak so well.

POSTURE AND MOVEMENT

Your bodily action can serve you well or betray you even before you speak. You begin communicating to your hearers when they catch sight of you. You make a certain impression on them. If you shuffle up to the front, or if you go up with a belligerent air, or if you sit on a platform and jiggle about, the impression will not be favorable.

When you have finished speaking, you have not finished *communicating* until you no longer are in view. Many novices at speaking scurry from the front as soon as they finish a speech, or they sidle away apologetically. What they have said can be undone. Some speakers are in such a hurry to escape from view that they begin leaving before they stop speaking.

Walk to the platform and from it with an easy, confident gait. Be an actor, if you have to. Though your heart is pounding and your legs are shaking, be an actor, and walk with confidence.

How should you stand, or sit, when you speak? Stand or sit comfortably. In general, be erect, but not stiff. You are not on military review. Pull your abdomen in, and your shoulders will go back naturally, also your posterior will be drawn in. Pull your abdomen in and everything else will take care of itself.

When you stand, see that you do not rock back and forth. Put one foot a little ahead of the other, and you will be unable to rock. More than one speaker teetering on a single axis, which you have when the two feet are exactly parallel, has stumbled.

The situation may be such that you do not stand exactly, neither do you sit in a chair. You put one leg on a chair or you sit on a table or you hunch across a speaker's stand—anything to be informal. Any posture is acceptable that helps you in communication. In many small group situations, erect standing is too formal.

Suppose you are explaining to a small group how a tiny transistor radio works. You could sit down on the desk and have your audience close to you. It would be better *not* to stand in this situation. Thus, whenever you have a small audience and the topic requires the nearness of everyone, or when the occasion is informal and you want to talk with intimate directness, sit on the desk, or in a chair as in committee or group discussion.

When the situation calls for sitting, be comfortable. But don't be a slack bag of bones. Slackness of body leads to slackness of mind and speech.

There are no rigid rules about bodily action, as there are none about speech in general, but there is an all-important practical principle: Whatever is right for the particular situation, that is, whatever works the best, determines what you should do. But this means, too, that you have to study the arts of speech, you have to know the things you can do before you choose *the* thing to do.

How about a speaker's stand or lectern? Use it if it doesn't become a psychological crutch. If you do not *have* to use it for your personal security, then you may use it. Too often the novice grabs hold of the stand and never lets go. Or he may lean upon it as though bowed by the weight of centuries. The lectern can be a help; too often it is a hindrance. It can be just a place where you put your notes; it can be a strategic center of operations for the seasoned speaker who moves to one side of it for a while, then to the other, standing behind it now and then too. Sometimes before a large audience, when a public address system is required, the speaker's freedom of movement is drastically curtailed. But if he has learned to do without a lectern, he will use it skillfully if he has to use it. He won't depend on it too much; he will not be glued to his notes which are on it; he will be able to gesture.

Avoid These Postures

1. The *concave chest*. This has as its inevitable corollaries the convex stomach and the retracted chin. It suggests a disregard for physical fit-

ness and appearance. It is not uncommon among intellectuals. Women who think they are too tall tend to develop it. It makes for limpness of personality.

2. The *swivel hip*. The weight of the body swivels on one hip or the other. One leg is markedly ahead of the other. The stomach protrudes. In advanced cases, the eyes glaze, the cheeks hang loose, the mouth droops. No positive message emanates from this posture. The force of the contortion throttles expression.

3. The *double knee bend*. I saw this posture beautifully executed by a superintendent of schools in a western city. It starts out with a feint as the person gets on tiptoes, then the feet flatten and the knees bend outward critically. It is virtually an acrobatic feat requiring the utmost precision and aplomb, for the knees stretch so far apart—at least in the case of the superintendent—that one wonders if there is any hope. But this superintendent did the trick often. People laughed and he thought he was funny. He *was* funny.

4. The *stiff neck*. This is found among the severe, the correct, the strait-laced. It is often associated with ultra-precise pronunciation. The whole body is rigidly erect. The all-encompassing inhibition allows but little gesture and facial expression.

5. The *pacer*. This is the non-stop walker. Back and forth he goes. Some walking from one place to another on the platform is effective. When the novice tries this technique of bodily action, he often overdoes it. In the learning process overdoing is a common stage. But there is also the veteran pacer. He is hard to restrain.

FACIAL EXPRESSION

One of the common causes of poor audience response is lack of eye contact. If you look at the ceiling most of the time or at the floor or out of the window or at your notes, your listeners will grow restless and inattentive. The speaker who cannot look at his audience ends up losing it.

You may have been advised: look just above the heads of listeners. This is supposed to make you less nervous. Avoid such indirection; it makes your audience nervous and it does not ease you. Again, your *eye* may look at the audience, but you do not. This is a common fault among chronic verbatim memorizers; the eyes are on the audience but the mind is on the next word or phrase of a manuscript.

The best speaking manner is the conversational manner. Talk as if you were talking with your friends. Be informal, be direct with your hearers, look them in the eyes. If the audience is large and you cannot

look everybody in the eye, concentrate on segments, swinging from one
segment to another. If you have notes, possibly detailed ones, you will
necessarily break your eye contact once in a while. But it should be *once
in a while.*

Facial expression looms large in the beautification of political candidates. Syd Simons, of the Make-up Artists and Hair Stylists Local 849,
in Chicago, was retained by the Republicans to apply his art to the faces
of their speakers at the 1960 national convention. Although Nixon at
first demurred to cosmetic treatment because "politicians aren't actors,"
he yielded to Simons' "purely clinical approach" and allowed his eyebrows to be thinned down. "Your eyebrows," said Simons to Nixon,
"are your greatest enemy. They bristle like John L. Lewis' brows. With
those deep eyes of yours, you look mean even when you smile." When
Nixon gave his acceptance speech his eyebrows had almost disappeared.

The depilation of Nixon's eyebrows did not extend to the head of
John F. Kennedy, although here too a shearing took place, in order to
make the man look less like a boy.

If hair removal from eyebrows or head can help to win or lose an
election, can we discount the importance of facial expression?

YOU CAN IMPROVE YOUR VOICE

You have seen a big burly fellow and have done a double take when
you heard him speak, for his voice was high and thin. You have heard
over the telephone the voice of a little girl until you are told by that
voice that this is Miss Roe, Mr. Jones's secretary. You have heard voices
that grate on your nerves, voices that express impatience, impertinence,
cockiness, sullenness. You have heard voices that indicate lack of education or lack of self-confidence or lack of interest.

The *New York Times* article on the English secretary observed: "Her
arrival does nothing whatever to soothe any troubled waters of the Atlantic but a great deal to soothe the boss, who likes the sound of her
voice on his telephone, and typing and shorthand be damned." But you
don't have to depend on England for well-spoken help. See what the
New York Telephone Company has done. Its exchange operators are
unfailingly courteous and easy to listen to. The company insists on
pleasant voices and offers a training course to get them. Shakespeare
says of one of his heroines: "Her voice is low, soft, and gentle, an excellent thing in a woman." Not all women should strive for exactly
Shakespeare's ideal of a voice, for in the competitive climate of todays'
business and professional world the voice of crisp decision is sometimes

needed. Yet many a domestic fracas would not have happened if that voice of crisp authority had been left in the office. This goes for men, too. Many a man's frayed nerves resound in a barking voice. He comes home and barks at his wife and barks at his children and then everybody starts to bark at each other.

Many of you remember the voice of Franklin Delano Roosevelt. You remember Inauguration Day, March 4, 1933. It was a desperate time. The Great Depression was at its worst. Over the radio that March 4 came a voice that braced us all, that filled us with confidence. The words too were inspiring, "We have nothing to fear but fear itself." But the words were no greater than that grand voice.

Many of you also remember the stirring voice of Winston Churchill in his wartime speeches. It epitomized the invincible courage, the massive determination, of the British people. Is it too much to say that here was a voice that set at naught the *Luftwaffe*?

I do not mean to say that your voice will make or break you, although it could. There are people who succeed in speechmaking in spite of their voices. They have other virtues that stand them in good stead. But a good voice will always *help* you.

Voice can be analyzed according to four main attributes: pitch, intensity, rate, and quality. Pitch is the highness or lowness of a tone; intensity is degree of loudness or carrying power; rate is speed of utterance; quality is the property of a voice that distinguishes your voice from someone else's, it depends on resonance. Resonance is what happens to the tones that vibrate from your vocal cords. The vibrations are reinforced in your throat, mouth, nose, and sinuses. How the vibrations are reinforced, or not, depends on the size, shape, and state of health of throat, mouth, nose, and sinuses.

The major voice faults are these:

Faults of Pitch

1. *Too high.* This may be because of a habit that started long ago. It may be the expression of taut nerves; the vocal cords tense up. To some extent it may be the effect of vocal cords that are short.

2. *Too low.* This is not as common as a pitch too high. It is often associated with the so-called guttural quality. It may be the result of misdirected zeal; someone tries too hard to acquire a low voice. A low voice is not necessarily an asset.

3. *Monotony*. This is a common fault. You may have only a two or three tone range. Monotony of pitch goes along with monotony of intensity and rate. The lack of range and flexibility makes for dullness, puts hearers to sleep.

Faults of Intensity

1. *Too loud*. You may be too loud for the size of the room. You may resort to this type of emphasis too often. You are so loud so much that you are called bombastic.

2. *Too quiet*. How often we've all been in audiences when cries of "Louder" shatter the peaceful air. Many theatergoers and dramatic critics have complained about the cult of naturalism in acting which makes actors indifferent to being heard.

3. *Monotony*. You may be loud too much of the time or quiet too much of the time. In either case, nothing is emphasized. Your ideas and phrases are all on the same level of minor importance. To be able to use all the kinds and degrees of intensity from a whisper to a shriek is the goal to work toward. Not that the shriek has much place in speech but if you can do a good shriek, it implies that you are adept in voice control.

Faults of Rate

1. *Too fast*. Some people talk so fast they can't pronounce words accurately. Some people just naturally talk faster than others. Such people in speaking should for the sake of emphasis slow down now and then. They should not try to slow down their basic rate unless it is clearly too rapid. A great American preacher of the late nineteen century, Phillips Brooks, had a very rapid rate. He tried to speak more slowly but could not without causing himself confusion and distress. His rate was so much a part of his temperament that he could not change it.

If you tend to talk rapidly, you should be more careful in pronunciation. Bear down on the individual sounds. Walter Winchell is a fast talker but his enunciation is vigorous and exact.

2. *Too slow*. Sometimes a speaker talks so slowly that his listeners fill in words for him aloud. If your rate is so slow that your audience gets impatient with you, speed up now and then.

3. *Monotony of rate.* Fast or slow too much of the time cancels out emphasis just as monotony of pitch and intensity does.

4. *Failure to use pause.* I include this as a fault of rate because pause is a powerful device that most speakers overlook. With a little practice, you can acquire facility in the use of it. Pause is not the same as hesitation. Pause is the device of a purposeful speaker. You can pause before or after a word or phrase that you aim to highlight. If you pause before, you arouse suspense; if you pause after, you give time to let something sink in.

Faults of Quality

1. *The nasal.* Too much resonance takes place in the nose. You may have heard the nasal twang of New England, the nasal clang of the Bronx, and the nasal drawl of southern Indiana. You can often reduce nasality by opening your mouth wider when speaking or by working out exercises to lower your pitch.

2. The *denasal.* There is too little resonance in the nose or none at all. If you have a bad cold and your nose is all stuffed up, you will have denasality. The *m* and *n* sounds and combinations will be damped out. Chronic adenoids are also a factor. A twisted septum bone in the nose may be responsible, also allergies. Anything that clogs up the nose causes denasality. Perhaps you should see a physician.

3. *Infantilism.* This is a high, thin, over-nasal voice. It makes a woman sound like a little girl. It makes a man sound effeminate. If you have a tendency to infantilism, begin now talking on a low pitch level. See how low you can get; then go up two or three tones and talk from there. And *practice, practice. Think* full tones. I say *think* because you should have the mental image of full tones. If you *think* them, they will come more readily. Read aloud and try for organ tones. Use all of your mouth; let sounds fill it.

4. The *guttural.* This is harsh and unnaturally deep in pitch. It can be the result of persistent misuse of the voice, which in turn can be the result of nervous strain. The main factor may be physical—infected tonsils, heavy smoking, heavy drinking, or nodes on the vocal cords. See a doctor if this type of trouble persists. But you might first try to relax; this is easier said than done. This book is not the place for psychotherapy, so I shall not prescribe treatment but what I have said earlier about sensible attitudes toward yourself as a speaker and a human being also applies here.

The *sepulchral* quality is closely related to the gutteral but is not so severe in its throat scratching. It is not so close to a growl as the guttural. It is the quality of the ghost of Hamlet's father.

5. *Hoarseness* or *huskiness*. This is often the result of "nerves" or misuse of the voice. People who speak a great deal may develop huskiness because they do not allow time for irritated vocal cords to heal. Fatigue can cause it. Nodes on the vocal cords can cause it. A cold or sore throat can cause it. Smoking or drinking may; you have heard of the "whisky voice." But of all the possible causes, the most common one is excessive tension. Therefore, cultivate the so-called "open throat"; this is a relaxed throat. But if you can't relax all over, it is hard to relax the throat. So it is a matter of your general outlook, your state of mind. Yet *thinking* the open, relaxed throat may induce generalized relaxation. Try it.

6. *Shrillness* or *stridency*. This is first cousin to hoarseness or huskiness. For again it is tension that is the villain of the piece. Shrillness is common among overwrought women. And stridency is common among overwrought men. You find it at the Chicago Wheat Pit and the New York Stock Exchange. You find it among those who have the Broadway stomach. Relax. Relax. Relax.

7. The *metallic*. This is first cousin to the strident. The sound is harsh and raspy.

8. The *aspirate*. This, for a change, may be the result of too much relaxation. The mouth and the throat are excessively lax, lacking muscular tone. And so the vocal cords are lax too, letting too much air through in relation to the sound produced. Again, however, the cause may be organic, nodes on the vocal cords, for instance. But if you do sound aerated, try first tensing up a bit. You may be so loose and slack around the mouth and throat that just the act of speech is a problem. Tense up, then, that is, tone up. Are you a man or a jellyfish?

Exercises and Corrective Measures

1. *How to find your best pitch level.* Your *habitual* pitch level, the one you ordinarily use, may be on the average either too low or too high against your *natural* pitch level which is the level that nature intends for you. This is the level which is determined by the length and thickness of your vocal cords. One dependable way of finding your best average pitch level is to start with the lowest tone that you can get to and then go up—*do, re, me,* etc.—tone by tone to the highest possible tone, in-

cluding falsetto. Count the total number of tones in this range and then from the bottom go up one-fourth of the number; this tone, one-fourth up, will be about your best natural pitch level. Practice this level. If possible, work with a recording device. A disc record or a tape is not indispensable but it helps. It enables you to detach yourself from yourself. You can listen to yourself objectively.

2. *How to develop flexibility*. The only way to develop vocal flexibility is to practice exercises that stress changes in pitch, intensity, rate, and quality.

One type of exercise is to work on material that forces flexibility upon you, like Patrick Henry's "Give me liberty or give me death" speech, or the following "nose speech" from Edmund Rostand's play, *Cyrano de Bergerac*. Cyrano is a brave, gallant, poetic fellow who has, however, a remarkably long nose. Highly sensitive, he allows no one to comment on the nose. But a foppish character recklessly does, saying: "You—your nose is—nose is—very large." Cyrano then states and illustrates many other, better, ways to describe the nose.

The piece requires much vocal variation: rapid to slow rates including pauses, high to low pitches, loud to soft intensities, and changes of quality. In quality, for instance, when Cyrano does the "Countrified" way of describing his nose, you might give his words with a nasal twang or a guttural sound. When he does the "Pedantic" way, try a sort of hollow, chesty sound.

Remember, this is a practice selection. For the particular purpose, vocal variety, there is none better. Try different techniques for each stated way of describing the nose: "Friendly," "Inquisitive," "Countrified," "Pedantic," etc.

And so to Cyrano's speech:

                                                No, young man.
That is somewhat too brief, You might say—Lord!—
Many and many a thing, changing your tone,
As for example these:—aggressively:
"Sir, had I such a nose I'd cut it off!"
Friendly: "But it must dip into your cup.
You should have made a goblet tall to drink from."
Descriptive: " 'Tis a crag—a peak—a cape!
I said a cape?—'tis a peninsula."
Inquisitive: "To what use do you put
This oblong sheath; is it a writing-case

Or scissors-box?" Or, in a gracious tone:
"Are you so fond of birds, that like a father
You spend your time and thought to offer them
This roosting-place to rest their little feet?"
Quarrelsome: "Well, sir, when you smoke your pipe
Can the smoke issue from your nose, without
Some neighbor crying, 'The chimney is a-fire'?"
Warning: "Be careful, lest this weight drag down
Your head, and stretch you prostrate on the ground."
Tenderly: "Have a small umbrella made,
For fear its color fade out in the sun."
Pedantic: "Sir, only the animal
Called by the poet Aristophanes
'Hippocampelephantocamelos'
Should carry so much flesh and bone upon him!"
Cavalier: "Friend, is this peg in the fashion?
To hang one's hat on, it must be convenient."
Emphatic: "Magisterial nose, no wind
Could give thee all a cold, except the mistral."
Dramatic: " 'Tis the Red Sea when it bleeds!"
Admiring: "What a sign for a perfumer!"
Poetic: "Is't a conch; are you a Triton?"
Naïve: "When does one visit this great sight?"
Respectful: "Let me, sir, pay my respects.
This might be called fronting upon the street."
Countrified: "That's a nose that is a nose!
A giant turnip or a baby melon!"
Or military: "Guard against cavalry!"
Practical: "Will you put it in a raffle?
It surely, sir, would be the winning number!"
Or parodying Pyramus, with a sob:
"There is the nose that ruins the symmetry
Of its master's features: the traitor blushes for it."
My friend, that is about what you'd have said
If you had had some learning or some wit;
But wit, oh! most forlorn of human creatures,
You never had a bit of; as for letters
You only have the four that spell out "Fool"!

You do not have such drastic vocal contrasts in most speaking; but most speaking for projection of meaning requires much more flexibility than you are able to give it. Therefore, practice the radical changes of pitch, intensity, rate, and quality. Practice these maximum changes so that when you speak you at least have the minimum—the minimum necessary for good communication.

Other selections that are excellent for practice in vocal variety are:

"The Walrus and the Carpenter" by Lewis Carroll

"Jabberwocky" by Lewis Carroll

"The Rime of the Ancient Mariner" by Samuel Taylor Coleridge

"The Raven" by Edgar Allen Poe

"The Tell-Tale Heart" by Edgar Allen Poe

"The Pied Piper of Hamelin" by Robert Browning

"General William Booth Enters into Heaven" by Vachel Lindsay

"The Congo" by Vachel Lindsay

"Chicago" by Carl Sandburg

"Jesse James" by William Rose Benét.

Hamlet's advice to the players: "Speak the speech, I pray you. . . ."

Macbeth's soliloquy: "Is this a dagger which I see before me . . ."

Some of these selections will undoubtedly tax you, as they also tax seasoned performers. But they will tax you into awareness of what you can do with your voice. The selections are emotionally vibrant. They would move stones to utterance. They compel the voice to respond. Practice with at least half of them and you will find that in your day to day speaking you become more expressive.

READING AND SPEAKING

Many a person speaks quite well until he comes to material that he needs to read and then he turns into an essay talking. He may need to read testimony, statistics, poetry; whatever it is, it seems to overcome him. He becomes stiff, mechanical, monotonous. He chose the material because of its importance in illustration or proof, yet he fails to convey its importance.

Learn to read as you speak, with equal variety and emphasis. Practice does it.

Look at the situations in which reading proficiency is essential. If you are a teacher, you frequently have to read aloud. If you are an English teacher, you are a misfit unless you can read effectively the many passages from literature in your year's work. Many cities and states require for teaching licenses evidence of reading skill.

Have you ever attended a convention, the specialized kind, where papers are read? Have you seen how the delegates walk in and out of a room where the drones are at work? Even the specialists can't stand a session for more than a reader or two.

Have you attended a business meeting where reports are read? How often the treasurer or a committee chairman puts us to sleep. Or have you attended a public hearing where key community groups express their views in the form of reports? Their mouthpiece may be a phonating cipher.

Think of television, in which the script or the teleprompter is often a necessity. See how some, as they pretend not to read, get that glazed, deadpan look from bondage to the teleprompter. Or see how the heads of some bob up and down as their owners try desperately to read and communicate; worse still, if the heads don't bob, they stay down, and all visual contact is gone.

Closed-circuit television is entering many fields. In the East an agency now exists to provide for doctors via closed-circuit television the latest discoveries in medical research. The busy doctor will find it hard to listen to dull reports. Throughout the country, closed-circuit television figures in education on all levels. There is an airborne television classroom in the Midwest that flies around and around broadcasting college instruction for credit. The most critical problem in educational television is to find teachers who have skill in speaking and reading before the camera.

The increasing scope of television will put a premium on training in the speech arts. So important has proficiency in speech for television become that, as in the eras past from ancient Greece and Rome to early twentieth-century America, the art of speech will hold a prime place in the education of an effective citizen. In eras past eloquence was the be-all and the end-all of the public man; it may be so again in an era where "public image" is a shibboleth.

There are situations in which a speaker chooses to read his speech. The problem is complicated by the "ghosted" speech. If it is hard to read effectively a speech of your own composition, it is almost impossible to read well the speech of a ghost. Not that it cannot be done, but it takes a lot of practice and skill. In this day of speeches that are read, in this day of "ghosted" speeches, it is important to learn to read well, to read so well that you do not seem to be reading, that you seem to be speaking.

Look at your audience while you read. You say, "How can I do this if I have to look at my script?" First, know your material so well that you don't have to spend most of your time with your eyes on the page; know the words and phrases that you want to emphasize; have clearly in mind the points that are the most important. Second, practice reading the material. Use techniques of voice and bodily action to stress key words and phrases (see sections on voice and bodily action). And re-member, read the material, except perhaps for poetry and dramatic se-lections, as if you were speaking it. Get out of the rut of assuming that words to be read will take care of themselves.

"How do I know I'm doing it right?" Here are some practical sug-gestions. Get hold of a tape recorder; rent, borrow, or buy one; listen to yourself speaking and to yourself reading; practice until the *speaking* you and the *reading* you are one and the same person. Experiment with different ways of emphasis: by increasing loudness or by whispering, by speaking each word in an important phrase or sentence with utmost care, by sharp contrasts of pitch from one phrase or sentence to another.

"How shall I hold the script or the sheet of paper or the note card when I read it?" If you have a speaker's stand, you can perhaps adjust the height so that when you put the reading matter down, it will not be so far down that you have to get special lenses to read it. Adjust the level of the stand so that the change from looking at your material to looking at your audience is at a minimum. But do not raise the stand so much that it hides your face.

Suppose you have no stand. Then hold the sheet or card outward and at an angle that will enable you easily to look up and at your audience. Do not hold the sheet or card against your stomach or chest so that you have to strain your neck to read it. Again, do not hold it so far out that your arm soon tires.

If you have a speaker's stand, use it part of the time, if you wish. Hold the material part of the time. If you are quoting from a heavy book, the stand may be essential. As in speaking, so in reading, the stand is a help but not a crutch. The seasoned speaker or reader is the master, not the slave, of the stand.

How much gesture should you have in reading? The answer: about the same as in speaking. Of course, if you hold the material, you are somewhat limited in freedom of gesture with both hands. But if one hand is free, use it.

In addition to gesture and voice in emphasis, you can call attention to an important phase of your material by introducing it with "Now get this" or "I think this is very significant" or "The next point is particu-larly interesting." Again, you may repeat a phrase or sentence. The speaker when he reads should take particular pains to point up impor-tant parts for the simple reason that the temptation is strong to let the words fend for themselves.

The presentation of statistics is always a problem, more so in reading than in speaking because the reader tends to go too fast. Go slow, go slow. The more complex the figures, the slower you go.

To keep the matter you read from being a mere jumble of words, you should work on dividing it into sensible units, groups of words that logically go together. Take the sentence just written. It breaks up into units as follows (vertical lines mark out the units, italics show special stress):

"To keep the matter you *read* / from being a mere *jumble* of words, / you should work on *dividing* it / into *sensible units,* / *groups* of words / that *logically* go *together.*" Use this method in analyzing and practicing the material you read. Where you want to indicate extra-special stress, use double horizontal lines.

Punctuation can give you the cues to meaning. Suppose you want to quote John Doe: "The best way to quit smoking is—to quit." The dash indicates that John Doe intends to set apart and emphasize "to quit." If you are to convey John Doe's meaning accurately, you will need a marked pause before "to quit." But if the sentence did not have a dash, and yet you felt that a pause was needed for adequate emphasis, you would have a perfect right to read it that way. The pause, a potent but underused technique of emphasis, is for the reader to use whenever he sees fit.

An exclamation mark immediately connotes strong feeling; it can also mean sarcastic or ironic intention. In the latter case the stress might be quite gentle: "Yes, indeed, the surest way to get rich is to be a teacher!" The stress could also of course be quite drastic; it would depend on the context of the sentence, the temper of the author, and the temper of the reader. In such a sentence as the following, however, there is no doubt about the degree and kind of emphasis: "Fire! Fire! My house is on fire!"

Yet punctuation can be a shifty-eyed guide to meaning. Some authors eschew the dash altogether; others, italics. Some use few or no commas; others use many. Some like semicolons where others like periods. Some few, among poets, use no punctuation at all. So, when it comes right down to it, you are the arbiter, the one who makes final decisions about shades of meaning.

THE COMMON SENSE OF PRONUNCIATION

Elegance is out. Punctilio is out. One sensible test of pronunciation is whether it conforms with the everyday usage of most of the educated people in your community. If it calls attention to itself, either by being sub-standard or by being ultra-precise, it confuses what you say with what you seem to be. In the one case you seem to be half-educated; in the other, you seem to be half-human. The precisionist always seems to be out of touch with humanity. In either case, what you have to say suffers. If you seem to be half-educated, your thinking is suspect; if you seem half-human, you have little to say of practical worth.

A second sensible test of pronunciation is its instant intelligibility. If you slur words or misplace syllable accents or utter inaccurate vowel or consonant sounds, you run the risk of not being instantly understood. This means a bottleneck in the path of meaning; if one word puzzles, others that follow it clot up to cause confusion. The trouble might be a regional variant. I once stayed for a summer with a native family in Cohasset, Massachusetts. For dinner one night there were steamed crabs. I understood the lady of the house to say to her husband, "They're shot." Just in from the Midwest where sea crabs were scarce, I exclaimed, "What! Do you shoot crabs?" The woman had used a localism of the Boston area; "shot" for *short*, to a Midwesterner, was quite a gap. When I returned to the Midwest for a visit a few years later, a friend said, "Where did you get that accent and what's happened to your r's?"

If you can be readily understood in all parts of the country, which is the objective of performers on radio and television networks, you have met the highest practical standard of diction—if you aim to do business in all parts of the country. But if you are content where you are, what do you care if tourists or outlanders don't understand you. Suppose you are a native of that proud city, Charleston, South Carolina. "Charlestonese," says *Time*, April 11, 1960, "is not an intelligible distortion of the American language in the sense that the dialects of Boston, Brooklyn and Davenport, Iowa, are. It pays the merest thank-you-ma'am to Webster's English, draws a lot of its vigor and flavor from Gullah, an African slave dialect still spoken by the White and Negro populations of the rice islands along the South Atlantic littoral, adds a touch of Huguenot French and a dash of regional accent that is as deep-rooted and mysterious as the brooding cypresses. Confronted with Charlestonese, philologists tremble." So in Charleston you would say, and real Charlestonians would get you instantly, "torsts" for *tourists*, "tren" for *train*, "plen" for *plane*, "air" for *ear*, "arm" for *I am*, "coined" for *kind*, "hot" for *heart*, "jell" for *jail*, "hell" for *hill*. "Minuet" for *You and I have eaten*. A woman from Manhattan had a hard time following a Charleston girl who said, "Min Wretched, after a lett dett, were goin' on the tren to Flettruck on Leebadee." How easy it would have been for the Manhattanite if the girl had said, "Richard and I, after a late date, are going on the train to Flat Rock on Labor Day."

Since you are a Charlestonian, it would be useless to tell you to mind your tongue. Moreover, why should you? You are not going to leave Charleston for long; you work and play in Charleston; and since you are instantly understood there and you speak the language of the educated, that's all that matters. If you do visit elsewhere, up "Nawth," for instance, who cares if the damnyankees don't follow you.

But the practical standards set by community usage may not do if you wish to teach or go on the stage, go into television or public relations, or into any other activity where you have to meet and talk to many people. The largest department store in Brooklyn, Abraham and Straus, gives an exacting speech test to applicants for jobs. The Board of Education of the City of New York tests prospective teachers by high speech standards. The stage and television demand your best in diction and voice, though that often means you have to be skilled in dialects and jargons and even in substandard speech. You could not portray the characters of *Tobacco Road* unless you were versed in illiterate talk.

The main concern here, however, is with the usage that meets two practical standards: instant intelligibility and acceptability to the educated in your community.

Most faults in diction and pronunciation result from (1) lazy lips, (2) fast talk, (3) ignorance, (4) local influence. Lazy lips and fast talk often go together. But so do lazy lips and slow talk. If your lips are slack, it is impossible to make sounds that are clear and accurate. Begin now to practice a vigorous attack on the syllables and sounds of words. Take pains to pronounce each sound emphatically. If your trouble is lazy lips, you may think when you practice vigorous enunciation that you are overdoing it while in reality you are only doing what others do naturally. Take five or ten minutes each day for a month to read aloud; mouth the syllables and sounds meticulously. Don't worry about being overprecise; in actual talk you won't be. You have had too long the habit of lazy lips ever to sin at the opposite extreme. You need never worry about prissiness.

If your habit is fast talk, the obvious thing is to slow down. And I do mean *slow down*. Slow down and bear down on syllables and sounds. Again, practice five or ten minutes a day reading aloud with utmost care. And watch your daily talk for a month. You will be surprised at the improvement a little systematic attention will effect.

Ignorance as a cause of poor pronunciation means two things: (1) that you are not aware of your faults, (2) that you are not familiar with a dictionary.

Check your pronunciation for types of errors in elementary words. An accumulation of little mistakes can misrepresent you: it suggests slipshod education or an untidy mind. You may consistently drop the *th* in final *ths* words like *months, widths,* and *truths;* the *t* in final *sts* words like *mists* and *lasts;* the final *t* in word pairs like *kept going* and *just because.* You may substitute incorrect consonant sounds for correct as *s* for the sound *z* in *because, was,* and *runs; z* for *s* in *gas* and *brass; sh* for *ch* or *tch* in *cheap, such,* and *stretch; ch* for the *j* sound in *bridge* and *edge.* Or you may substitute *b* for *p* in words like *apple* and *cap; d* for *th* in *that, without,* and *other; t* for *th* in *fourth* and *mouthful; t* for *d* in *muddle* and *riddle; d* for *t* in *letter, little,* and *metal.* These words are only two or three cases of large categories.

Again, you may use incorrect vowel sounds. You may say "bed" for *bad,* "sped" for *spade* or "let" for *late,* "pal" for *pail* or "tal" for *tale,* "luck" for *lock* or "knuck" for *knock,* "buck" for *book* or "ruff" for *roof.* Or you may pronounce the *o* in the *com* of *come, comfort* and *company* like the *o* in *comma.* That's one of the troubles with the English language: words often have to sound different than they look. The *o* in these *com's* should have the sound of the *u* in *must.*

Local influence has its specific regional impacts all over the country. So in Southern Indiana you will hear "far" for *fire,* "tar" for *tire,* "condeshun" for *condition.* In Texas you will hear "pin" for *pen,* "agin" for *again,* and a flat, nasal *a* in such words as *man, ask, laugh,* and *calf.* In Boston, you will hear "dater" for *data,* "idear" for *idea,* "Bastin" for *Boston.* And in dear old, abused Brooklyn, you may still hear "erl" for *oil,* "berl" for *boil,* "foin" for *fine,* "Oive" for *I've*—but not so much as you may think.

Now that you know the what's and why's of faulty pronunciation, we can get down to the practical business of correction. Keep in mind, we are for usage that makes for instant intelligibility and for social acceptability among the educated of the community in which you live and work.

The steps in the correction of faults are as follows:

1. You are made aware of the fault. You hear it when you make it.

2. You know how to eliminate the fault. Sometimes you need only be aware of it and it goes. Other times you need to know what to do with tongue and lips, jaws and teeth.

3. You practice what is correct. You also deliberately commit the error you want to remove, for this makes you mindful of the differences in sound and physical sense between what is correct and what is incorrect.

4. By all means, begin now the dictionary habit. When in doubt, go to the dictionary; also at times when not in doubt, for ignorance has a way of removing doubts.

9 SPEECHES FOR SPECIAL OCCASIONS

SPEECHES FOR SPECIAL OCCASIONS ARE LIKE SPEECHES TO persuade or inform. The same principles of content, structure, language, and delivery apply. But there are special characteristics of mood, material, and length to consider. For instance, the speech of introduction specializes in the experience and distinctions of a person, with now and then comment on the significance of his topic. The speech should be as brief as circumstances permit: the better known the speaker you introduce, the shorter the introduction. I once introduced the late Guthrie McClintic, the Broadway director, at a student convocation at Indiana University. I worked hard on the introduction. It was meaty, well-wrought, and six minutes long. When I finished giving it, Mr. McClintic arose and said: "I have nothing to add."

In the speech of introduction you advertise the merits of a person, you sell him. You set forth his qualities with concrete, interesting material. Sometimes the humanizing anecdote is just the thing. A distinguished executive of a television network was introduced by a long-time friend. Said the friend, among other things: "I knew Mr.——when we were kids. He lived right across the street from me. One afternoon just after I received a BB gun for my birthday, I saw Mr.——(then called 'Pete') across the street. I was on our porch. I took careful aim and pinked him where occasionally he had been spanked. The next afternoon as I walked up our porch steps I felt a sting where occasionally I had been spanked. Odd that we who shot each other are on the same platform."

The introduction should not give a person such an extravagant build-up that he is embarrassed. Praise him, yes, but don't make a superman of him. Particularly avoid saying, if he is to give an after-dinner speech: "Now we are to hear from one of the funniest men alive." You would dry up his humor, even if he were one of the funniest men alive.

It is hard to do but—try to avoid such expressions as: "It gives me great pleasure to" or "It is a great privilege and a great pleasure to." It may be what you say it is but, as with all clichés, the phrases seem empty and insincere.

The following speech of introduction was given at a meeting of the Executives' Club of Chicago on February 23, 1951, by its president, Thomas H. Coulter. He introduced Marguerite ("Maggie") Higgins, then a correspondent back from the Korean war front. The speech is notable for its specific matter, its clear-cut language free of cliché, its touches of humor and drama. It portrays a person who is at once an authority and an interesting human being. A fault, however, is its length.

When Maggie Higgins arrived at the Korean battlefront two days after the Communist invasion, she had no idea that her daring reporting would catapult her to international fame. Instead of writing headlines she herself became one almost overnight, when General Walker bounced her out of Korea with the advice that a war was no place for a woman.

She protested to General MacArthur that she was not working in Korea as a woman but as a war correspondent, and put up such a good front about why she should be at the front that he granted her a reprieve.

In spite of all her efforts to conceal her womanly attributes in baggy pants, oversize shirts and a solid covering of Korean dust, the GI's haven't been fooled and one admiring observer remarked, 'Maggie wears mud like other women wear makeup.'

Miss Higgins owes her physical properties to an Irish-American father and a French mother, who became a war bride after meeting her father as a combat flyer in World War I. Mr. Higgins became a globe-trotting businessman, which resulted in Maggie being born in Hong Kong. She spoke only French and Chinese until the age of twelve. After schooling in France, she attended the University of California where she graduated with honors.

She became a *Herald-Tribune* campus correspondent while working for her master's degree in journalism at Columbia, and in 1942 joined the paper's New York staff.

Two years later, Miss Higgins got the chance she had been asking for. Because of her fluency in French, the *Herald-Tribune* sent her to Europe as a war correspondent.

There she covered Buchenwald and reported the capture of Munich and the liberation of Dachau and Berchtesgaden. For the last two of these stories, she was given the New York Newspaper Women's Club award for the best foreign correspondent of 1945. The same year, at age twenty-four, she became chief of the paper's Berlin Bureau.

After three years of able postwar reporting in Germany, she became the *Trib's* Tokyo Bureau chief last June, and was one of the first reporters to get to Korea when the war started.

She has been at the fighting front almost continuously since then, and has retreated in defeat and advanced in victory from Pusan to the Manchurian border where she was trapped with the marines at the Changjin reservoir.

Her disregard for personal safety would have warmed the heart of Ernie Pyle. Once when she was not heard from for several days, it turned out that she had landed with the fifth wave of marines at Inchon, and stayed with them under intense mortar and machine gun fire until that beach was secured.

All this has made "news-chick" Higgins a sort of GI heroine, won her the universal affection of the troops, and endeared her to millions of readers.

The question of what makes Maggie run so hard and fast, fascinates her three hundred male competitors in Korea almost as much as the war itself. She has forced these who at first regarded her as an impudent upstart in the business of reporting battles to admit grudgingly that she was their match when it came to bravery and scoops.

She is a symbol of the courage and intelligence that sets apart the great war correspondent from the routine reporter.

We are privileged to hear her make her first public address.

Ladies and Gentlemen: Miss Marguerite Higgins.

THE M. C.

Someone who has several speakers to introduce on the same program can spend but little time on each. What he does say should be crisp and to the point. The M.C. who dawdles over each speaker dulls the whole occasion. While he should prepare a brief piece for each speaker, he should be in a state of alert for the something that comes up while the program is in progress. The skilled M.C. for a program of speakers can depart from his prepared patter for the spontaneous bit, just as does the M.C. in a nightclub.

Beware of trying too hard to be funny. You need not introduce every speaker with a joke or a wisecrack. Your job is not to make yourself out as a wit or a showman, it is to fix attention on the speakers.

The rule of brevity should not be enforced with equal severity for all speakers. A speaker may not be as well known to the audience as another or he may be a person whose distinction deserves more time. If you need data about a speaker, go to the various who's who publications. Or inquire if he has a personal data sheet. But you will have to be selective. Who's who accounts and personal data sheets in most cases tell all; you will choose only the items most significant.

You may be in charge of seating arrangements. Have a care for protocol. Unless there are special considerations, the speakers having the highest rank or office or social position are central on the dais or at the table. One special consideration would be the presence of men and women; then it would be wise to alternate them. Another would obviously be the honoring of someone of humble rank. You should introduce the speakers to each other, see that they are comfortable.

Remember to check the public address system, if one is necessary. See that those weird whistles and squeaks are gone. Better no public address system than one that acts up. If you have a speaker who prefers not to use one, turn it off.

If time limits for the speakers have been indicated, you may need to enforce them. You will of course do this with nice discretion. A tug at the sleeve is better than a kick in the shin.

SPEECHES OF PRESENTATION AND TRIBUTE

The speech of presentation attends a gift or an award to someone. It extolls the recipient for his virtues, achievements, and contributions. It ties up the particular gift or award with the interests and hobbies of a person. Usually a short speech—one not over five minutes long—it needs care. It can be dreary, uninspired twaddle. But it can be lively and appealing, if you fill each minute with concrete instance and human interest material, and if you have original touches here and there. An alumna of Brooklyn College was given an award of honor for outstanding achievements. The person making the presentation soberly set forth her impressive record and ended by saying: "All this, ladies and gentlemen, and a husband and four children, too." It was a fillip that brought down the house. At a similar occasion, a few years later, a speaker in presenting the award to the alumnus and renowned actor, Alfred Drake, called the recipient "Mr. Theater" and in telling how Drake got his start while an understudy for William Gaxton he quoted from a letter of Drake: " 'Gaxton graciously came down with the flu and I went on for him for one week.' " For his final words, the speaker again quoted from Drake's letter: " 'Maybe this all began back in Boy's High School when a Speech Teacher insisted I try out for the Semi-Annual Declamations Contest. I won—and I have a solid gold medal to prove it.' "

The speech of tribute, or the eulogy, is similar to the speech of presentation, but it is often longer and therefore offers greater possibilities for boredom. Use all your ingenuity at phrase making, all your knowhow in selecting material. You can eulogize anything: mother, country, martinis, dogs, boys, virtues.

The following speech, "Integrity: A Mighty Force," can be called a speech of tribute or a eulogy. It can be viewed as in praise of a virtue or the person who exemplifies the virtue. Newsman, author, and diplomat Henry J. Taylor presented it over the radio, one of 725 such speeches that he broadcast weekly from December, 1945, to December, 1956. In this speech, as in many of his others, Mr. Taylor shows his skill in the use of dramatic illustration.

Anything you and I can do to help restore faith in integrity it is our duty to do—and now.

This brings me to a personal story. I cannot tell you this story in an impersonal way because I lived through it.

The period covers 12 years. The scene is Chicago. The story began before the stock market crash of 1929.

Otto Schnering had started a candy-bar business in Chicago. Beginning in a small way, in 1916, he developed the business into a going concern by the early twenties. He called it the Curtiss Candy Company; and he originated the BABY RUTH candy bar.

Working round the clock—thinking, trying, risking, worrying, and always working—the Schnering team finally achieved national distribution of its BABY RUTH five-cent candy bars. They were on sale in every state in the Union.

This was accomplished by selling better quality at a lower price—the fundamental history of the entire American free opportunity system, which has made this country the most productive in all the world.

It was done, as well, by sacrificing current profits year after year in order to build tomorrow's business—likewise the essential history of capital development in our counrty.

By the late twenties, the small Curtiss company was no longer small. It had created a whole new five-cent-candy field for the American consumer. The company's needs for commodities had grown as the business grew. It needed more sugar, chocolate coating, peanuts, wrappers, boxes. As the sales went up and the company's employment rolls went up, by the thousands and thousands—more people working in the candy plants, more salesmen, more office workers—more and more money was needed by the management to keep going. Same story in any business.

Then the crash came in the world commodity markets. It came far ahead of the 1929 stock market crash in our country.

Raw materials from all over the world that the company had contracted for were no longer worth what the company had agreed to pay. People who had sold these things to Otto Schnering stood to lose a lot of money. They needed cash—and quickly.

But because he and his company had plowed their profits back into the business, the company couldn't pay these bills unless it could immediately collect its own bills due from its own customers. This couldn't be done.

The panic was on. On May 28, 1929, Otto Schnering called a meeting of the principal creditors.

I myself had started a business of my own, and eventually sold large quantities of supplies to the Curtiss Candy Company. Almost everything I had was tied up in its integrity. That's the point—its integrity.

The creditors' meeting was held in the ballroom of Chicago's Belmont Hotel—on a dull grey afternoon, as ominous outside as in the tense, packed atmosphere of that room.

Schnering was told not to come to that meeting. He was excluded, as was every member of the management team. Told to remain in the near-by main office and await the decision of bankruptcy, they were asked to wait there for news of who would succeed Schnering—take over the business built through a decade by men and women whose very success in increasing the business was about to break them, wash out their money and their hearts, and oust them from their jobs.

Up in the ballroom a decision had been reached by the creditors' meeting. The machinery would be sold. Dismissal notices would go to all employees. Any remaining debts would be abandoned as worthless. The company was through.

Then an amazing thing happened on the floor of the meeting. A man got up and made a little speech. What he said was not remarkable. The remarkable thing is what happened all over the ballroom.

"The Curtiss business ceases to exist without Otto Schnering and his loyal team," he said. "Any credit extended was extended to that management, not to some inexperienced committee. I have talked with Otto Schnering on this very day. Schnering said to me, 'You know we can't collect the amount due from our customers now. We can't pay your bills. It may take years to pull through. But if everybody will wait and is willing to help, I can see this awful time through and I'll dedicate my life to this job."

"That statement," the speaker went on, "is enough for me. The integrity of this business is the integrity of the people in it, the integrity of the management. I cast my lot with that integrity and with no other."

The speaker got no further. There was a rumble across the floor. One man after another called "Order! Order!" Men were standing to speak in every part of the room—to speak up and stand with Otto Schnering and the integrity of the team.

The majority of the creditors voted to let Schnering stay in. It took 12 years to clear away the financial problem. Day by day, month by month, year by year, dollar by dollar. From 8 in the morning until 8 at night—10 at night, 12, 1, 2, 3. No letup, no security for Schnering and his associates. Each day simply meant a chance for those men to take each problem, hour by hour, and see it through. Never was a payroll missed—never a penny defaulted. There never was a crack in the integrity of Otto Schnering.

As time went on, however, there was a crack in his health. He had given his life to this problem and his health suffered.

You see, even before the first year had passed, the depression struck. Every original problem of the management was multiplied. But the Curtiss Candy Company lived through everything and paid off every debt. The team won. Integrity won out—and nothing else but.

In 12 years every step had been retraced and the battle of integrity was over, and this great company is going great guns today. Last year it had the largest sales and largest profits in its history.

The years since this episode make much of it seem distant. And now my dear friend is dead. But the time that has passed has not changed the importance of such a performance. For there is never any change in honest principles. The good that men can do today by the example of integrity is the greatest good that can be done.

Otto Schnering passed away leaving you with the warm memories of a close friend which makes it so hard to believe that anyone we have ever loved is really gone, or that life itself is much more than a dream.

ACCEPTANCE, RESPONSE, FAREWELL, AND ANNIVERSARY

We are concerned here with speeches for such occasions as an anniversary, the acceptance of a nomination or an award, the farewell at the end of a period of service or at the departure of a friend or a colleague.

In most of the speeches, human interest material—stories, anecdotes, personal experiences—should predominate. The taste of the speaker is critical in the choice. At a retirement ceremony for a distinguished but mettlesome professor, there was a good deal of the raking over of old coals. Much bitterness and sarcasm were vented. An official of the university was introduced as one who was "if not sounding brass, at least tinkling cymbal" (was there a pun on *cymbal*?). When the time came for the retiring professor to speak, the question was, would he add to the tensions? In the past he had not been one to shrink from acrimony. But this time he was all smiles and gentle words. The wars were over. He touched on his battles in the halls of learning but he did so without venom. By forbearance and humor he rescued an occasion that had become rather grim.

A retirement or farewell function is not the time for discord. It is the time for good fellowship, for pleasantries, for appreciation of worth.

The acceptance of a nomination may be the occasion for a major policy speech. The occasion may call for a sober survey of problems and objectives; it certainly calls for an optimistic outlook. You would, of course, speak of the sharing of responsibilities and burdens; you would soft-pedal your own prowess. Modesty should pervade your words; this goes for all speeches of acceptance and response.

The occasion for an anniversary speech might be the Fourth of July, Lincoln's birthday, a golden wedding, Veteran's Day, Founder's Day. The speech should awaken or deepen appreciation; it should please or inspire, or both.

THE SPEECH OF WELCOME

The speech of welcome often gets stepchild treatment. It gets the hand-me-down phrases, "We are happy to have you here"; "Words cannot tell how proud we are to have you with us"; "It is our proud privilege to welcome you to this fair city." It gets these phrases and many more like them, but little else, in the five or ten minutes allotted. Throw away the clichés; dig into what the organization you are to welcome stands for; connect what it stands for with what your city or school, or whatever the host, stands for or values. Let this be the main substance of the speech. As in other speeches, make an outline. Illustrate, support, each point. Tax your talent for graphic language, for novel statement—"Los Angeles may no longer have angels, but it is close to starlets. Heaven is far above us, but Hollywood is right beside us."

The following speech of welcome is decidedly hypothetical as to facts and figures but does illustrate the type of speech.

Let us assume that the mayor of Duluth, Minnesota, a hay fever mecca, gives the speech to the Hay Fever Association of America, Inc., in any Duluth auditorium, any August 15 which is the official opening day of the hayfever season.

Fellow sufferers, I mean *fortunates*, I too have this ailment, I mean *condition*, that sets us apart from those insensitive people who, in the ragweed sections of the country, live without sneezing. As long as I can remember, I have had this condition—I suppose I still have it. I haven't noticed it since I moved here from Chicago twenty years ago. I am proud of my kinship with you. We are a special class.

The Hay Fever Research Board of the Duluth Chamber of Commerce after three years of arduous research has come up with some interesting findings on us. The average IQ of hay fever victims—I mean *fortunates*—is 5.8 higher than that of the public at large. Moreover, hay-feverites read more books than those other people. The average fortunate reads 2.4 books a month; the average unfortunate reads .36 of a book a month.

Certain specialists of cerebral processes even see a connection between respiratory sensitivity and genius. Dr. Adolphus Re, specialist in the left hemispherical lobe of the brain and now with the Duluth Chamber of Commerce, puts it this way, "If membranes are insensitive, brains are too."

The Hay Fever Research Board also finds our economic status higher than the general average. Do you know that the average annual income of hay fever sufferers—I mean *fortunates*—is $8,652 while that of other people is $6,407? Do you know that 78 per cent of us own our own homes compared to 57 per cent of those other people? And do you know that the typical hay-feverite has 1.36 cars while a typical other person has .78 of a car?

As one whose daily concern is with law and order, I am gratified to report also that the Hay Fever Research Board has found the crime rate among hay-feverites to be significantly lower than that of other people. In convictions for first-degree murder, there are 1.3 per 10,000 of us but 3.7 per 10,000 of those. In convictions for grand larceny there are 4.2 per 10,000 of us but 12.8 per 10,000 of those. "This is not surprising," declares Dr. Re, "because a sensitive membrane means a sensitive conscience."

For these reasons Duluth is proud to have you here again. Duluth wants you to know that her motels and hotels, her restaurants and stores, her theaters and nightclubs are ready and waiting for you. Make Duluth your August and September homes. Duluth bids you throw away your inhalants and your anti-anti-anti—kerchoo!—excuse me—histamines.

Who brought in that pollen? Some saboteur, no doubt, from the White Mountains of New Hampshire.

THE AFTER-DINNER SPEECH

The after-dinner speech need not keep everyone in stitches. It can be entertaining without being hilarious. It may be nostalgic; it may even bring a tear or two. It may deal in mystery and suspense. It may indeed have a serious purpose. It may aim to inform or persuade, but if it pleases or entertains or thrills, it does its proper work.

Sometimes the after-dinner speech is left to chance, as if it were something unworthy to attend to. Sometimes it is just a string of jokes without point. The best after-dinner speeches are carefully prepared; if someone makes a hit with an impromptu speech, it is ten to one that at some time he gave the subject special thought or gave a speech related to it. It was said of Winston Churchill by one of his critics that he gave the best years of his life to thinking up his spontaneous remarks.

Suppose you are to speak after dinner to a gathering of public relations men. You decide to spoof the ways in which people try to get the best of each other in an argument. The topic is perfect for your particular audience. You decide to give the speech a mock persuasive slant: you will urge your hearers to try out what you advise. You word your thesis "Five Ways to Win an Argument." You plan to begin by saying that the advice you are about to give is guaranteed to work in all situations except disputes with wives. Next you outline your speech: each way to win an argument is a sub-topic which you formulate in the terms of daily usage, as follows:

1. "Let's kick the ball around a little more," that is, you win by protracting the argument.
2. "Well, there are two schools of thought," meaning your school is better.
3. "We're really talking about the same thing," which prompts the reaction, "Yes, I guess we are."
4. "Let's see if I follow you; as I understand it, this is what you're saying." Your synopsis is your side of the argument. Only the sharpest opponent will see through this device.
5. "Try to see it my way." Which means, there is no other way.

If you are one of several after-dinner speakers, observe the time limits if such have been set. Observe a limit of your own if none has been set. A good rule to follow is this: if there is no strong reason to talk more than five minutes, don't. Better to err on the side of brevity than to have your listeners look at their watches.

10 GROUP DISCUSSION

DISCUSSION IS THE ART OF COOPERATIVE THINKING ALOUD. It could also be called the art of exchanging ideas without calling each other names. In a sense discussion is the opposite of debate. In the one you do not start out with a definite proposition, in the other you do; in the one you search for answers or solutions, in the other you have the answers or the solutions and you try to put them across. It would be fine if before we engaged in debate or propaganda we sat down with others and reviewed with an open mind all the aspects of a problem. Think of the ideal situation in which one did not arise to defend a proposition until he had subjected the whole matter to an impartial scrutiny! The trouble is, in a pressure-laden environment where personal, national, and international matters have to be settled with dispatch, the time for impartial scrutiny is precious little. Too often matters have to be settled by immediately taking a stand on an issue; this means debate, argument, persuasion, and propaganda.

Discussion would be the ideal instrument in a world where men and women were not human beings, where error and doubt could be easily dispelled, where truth existed for a certainty and could be readily found. In such a world, people need only sit down together to examine a problem; in a short time it would be resolved. But, alas, this is not to be. The best we can hope for is that when people do meet for discussion they do not make it an occasion mainly for the pushing of their special interests. In other words, we can hope that if discussion is to be the order of the day there should be a minimum of outright debate, persuasion, and propaganda.

Discussion stresses reflective thinking, that is, objective and informed thinking. The informed thinker knows what he knows and knows what he does not know and is ready to admit he does not know. The objective thinker realizes that a discussable problem has many aspects; he presents what he knows and listens carefully to what others seem to know. The objective thinker is after as much fact as possible; he is not a spur-of-the-moment man. The objective thinker is a reasoner; he knows how to reason (see earlier section on ways to reason); he can spot weaknesses in data and logic. He is not a prey to words (see section on words that hinder thinking); he is in control of words.

A discussion situation exists in committees, round-tables, seminars, panels, symposiums, and question and answer setups. When labor and management get together to negotiate a contract, discussion is the apparent means. Actually, debate is the means. Both parties start on the assumption that each party is out to get as much as he can. The process of negotiation may go on for a long time with the side effects of strikes, work stoppages, picketing, and violence. It would be ideal if the parties could start on the assumption that each party has something to offer and that only by calmly listening to each other can a just decision be reached. Even where the stakes are not purely matters of dollars and cents, objectivity is hard to come by. Try discussing religion or politics. And the halls of academe have many tales to tell of discussions where axes are ground and empires are built.

But if we keep in mind how easy it is to sin in discussion, maybe we can better resist temptation. Who of us is not a little prejudiced on just about anything? Who of us is not prone to sit in judgment—although some seem more prone than others. Who of us is without vested interest, special interest, personal interest? Who of us is safe from impulse and anger? The way to objective discussion is rocky and thorny, but if we know that it is and pretend no different, we can do as good a job of group thinking as it is possible for mortals to do.

The types of problems that come up for discussion are three: fact, value, policy. The problem of fact can be resolved only by finding as much usable fact as possible. The best way to attack such a problem is for experts to discuss it. The best way to decide on the relative merits of the killed-virus polio vaccine and the live-virus vaccine is for pathologists, bacteriologists, and physiologists to confer. Laymen should not try to answer this specialized question of fact. Since the experts themselves disagree, what would be the situation if laymen agreed? Take the question of cigarettes and lung cancer. Here, too, the specialists disagree. Yet this question is more in the realm of legitimate factual questions for laymen than the one on polio vaccines because the outcome of lay discussion of it does not have the immediate lethal possibilities that a lay decision on the vaccines could have. Moreover, there is much more material in the public domain on cigarettes and lung cancer than on live-virus and killed-virus vaccines.

Questions of fact which are definitely suited to the general citizenry are those that could yield satisfactory or practical answers now. Such questions might be:

1. What levels of take-home pay are necessary for houses that range from $20,000 to $35,000?
2. Is a five cent increase in the bus fares necessary?
3. What are the main causes of the high cost of living?
4. What are the differences between socialism and democracy?
5. What were the chief causes of the Civil War?

There are experts in these areas, too, but the areas are not so narrowly specialized, not so exacting in research qualifications, as to make them utterly inaccessible to the layman. Again, the questions are not so simple as to make the answers self-evident. There has to be leeway for interpretation and difference of opinion, else a question is not discussable. What would be the point of discussing the question, is the sun shining today? Or the question, are there more automobiles on the highways today than twenty-five years ago?

The question of value is similar to one of fact, only it allows for still more interpretation and difference of opinion. It has to do with "value judgments." Facts have to play a part in discussing a question of value but you might look for facts until the crack of doom and your files might be bursting with data, and there will still be plenty of room for differences of interpretation and evaluation. Whether John Doe or Richard Roe is the better candidate for president is ultimately decided not so much by the relentless pressure of facts as by personal preference which could be based on how a candidate combs his hair.

The following are questions of value:

1. Will the paintings of Picasso stand the test of time?
2. What is success?
3. Who is the more entitled to the Nobel Prize for literature: Robert Frost or Carl Sandburg?
4. Is woman's place mainly in the home?
5. Is honesty the best policy?
6. Is religion losing its hold on the young?

The policy question is directed to a solution for a problem. The emphasis is on what should be done.

Policy questions are:

1. What should be done about the rising cost of living?
2. Should bus fares be increased?

3. Should price supports for farm products be changed?
4. What should be done about the competition of Japanese products?
5. Should Communist China be admitted to the United Nations?

THE DISCUSSION PLAN

Discussion ranges all the way from the "brain storm" session and the "bull session" to the formal symposium. The "brain storm" approach applies the stream of consciousness method to the solution of problems. Let us assume, for example that ten of you meet in a room to "brain storm" the question, What can we do to stabilize price levels? There would be no chairman, no leader. Other than yourselves there would be only a fast writer who could put on the blackboard all your suggestions, your inspirations, as fast as you all made them. The aim of the brain storm session is to bring out in the open, without inhibition, anything that occurs to you on the general question. No one is to have any self-restraint with regard to freedom of expression. Speak out the instant something comes to you. If you all keep this up for twenty minutes, the blackboard, and a big one it must be, should be filled with ideas. Some of them may be quite sound and practicable. You don't assess them until the brain storm period is over. There are businesses that swear by this method. They claim that it makes for creativeness, that it draws out the latent originality of even the shy. The method may appall the orderly and make mad the precise, but if it works, who cares? And it does, says Madison Avenue, work.

The "bull session" is familiar to most of you. It may be, but usually is not, organized discussion. The participants are free to ramble as they please. Any informal, conversational group carries on a "bull session." Here, as in brain-storming, there is no leader as such; there may be a monopolist, but that is another matter.

The main concern of this section, however, is planned and orderly discussion. This means the devising of a topical scheme, or outline, for the members of a group to use in preparing for the discussion or in guiding their thinking during the discussion. A leader is thus assumed, who will be responsible for the preparation and distribution of the outline. It is a tentative outline, not to serve as a strait jacket, but to guide group thinking.

The outline depends on the type of question. If a policy question is to be discussed, the outline might run as follows:

What Should Be Done to Check Inflation?
I. Introduction

A. Definition of inflation
B. Historical background
    1. Conditions just before the Great Depression
    2. Conditions in Germany after World War I
C. Criteria of economic health
    1. Supply and demand not too far apart.
    2. Unemployment—except for unemployables and seasonal factors—non-existent.
    3. Increase of productivity does not outrun consumption.
    4. Stocks are not priced higher than their value.

II. What is the problem?
    A. Price index is rising steadily.
    B. Wages are rising steadily.
    C. Stocks, but for temporary recessions, are going up.
    D. Farm prices are artificially supported, while surpluses accumulate.
    E. Our economy is geared to the outlook of a cold war that might become hot.

III. What are possible solutions to the problem?
    A. Everyone should resolve to cut his purchases by 10 per cent for one year.
    B. Everyone should resolve to increase his savings by 10 per cent for one year.
    C. Farm prices should be allowed to seek their natural level.
    D. The escalator clause in labor contracts, which provides for automatic wage increases if the price index goes up, should be suspended for one year.
    E. Stricter regulations on installment buying should be invoked.
    F. "No down payment" arrangements on new houses should be abolished.

IV. What is the best solution or the best combination?
    A. Which solutions are workable?
    B. Which solutions would be supported?
    C. Which would strike at the heart of the problem?

V. What can we do now to put into effect the best solution or combination?

If the question to be discussed is one of value, this might be the outline:

Does Television Make or Reflect Public Taste?
  I. What did the craze for big prize quiz shows mean?
 II. What does the prevalence of Westerns mean?
III. What does the trend to plays of violence and cruelty signify?
 IV. What is the popularity of the Sunday "intellectual ghetto" shows?
  V. What is the popularity of the second, third, and fourth-run movies?
 VI. Is television advertising what the public wants?

A question of fact could be outlined as follows:

What Are the Effects of Television on the Reading Habits of Viewers?
  I. Are more books being read today per 1 million people than ten years ago?
 II. What is the average viewing time today of each person as compared to ten years ago?
III. Are more children checking out library books today than ten years ago?
 IV. What is the effect of television on attendance at movie houses; if viewing time is up and number of books read is up, what is cut—movie attendance?
  V. Are more comic books being read today than ten years ago; are comic books to be defined as books?

In the case of each outline above, the topics are but guideposts. They serve to stimulate and direct thinking both before and during discussion. If the group raises other points, the chairman should be ready to shift focus.

The plan of the discussion depends partly on the type: informal group, question and answer, panel, or symposium. The informal group may number as many as fifty or sixty participants, all seated if possible in a circle or rectangle so that they face each other. The question and answer type of discussion, which television has popularized in such programs as *Meet the Press* and *Face the Nation,* puts someone on the spot; the inquisitors fire questions at a victim. The panel discussion consists of a small group, three to nine members, with or without an audience. The panelists talk informally, they are well prepared, we hope, but they do not present set speeches. The symposium is relatively formal; there may be three to six members, each ready with a main speech, three to ten minutes long; there is always an audience. After the main speeches, the participants may have a period for an informal exchange of comments.

Whenever possible, the members of a discussion group should face each other; this makes for directness and closer attention. The symposium, however, which is primarily for the benefit of an audience, has a format in which the members do not face each other but face the audience. The question and answer type has questioners and questionee looking at each other. The informal group and the panel have the members in some circular or squarish formation so that they can all easily see each other.

QUALIFICATIONS AND BEHAVIOR OF MEMBERS OF A DISCUSSION GROUP

1. *Listen attentively*. If there is one bad manner that does the most to undermine cooperative, friendly relations, it is inattention. This covers a wide range of rudeness from the person who seems to be listening but indicates when he speaks that he has no idea of what you said, to the person who deliberately looks out the window or at the ceiling when you speak or who closes his eyes as if in sleep. Some there are, of course, who consciously practice the arts of distraction. They put up an ingenious front of inattention. Such persons should not pretend to be members of a discussion group; they should stay at home and talk to themselves.

Attentive listening is a mark of respect for others. It suggests to others that they are worth listening to. It encourages others to speak more freely, to "unbend." It creates a friendly atmosphere. Attentive listening is practical democracy at its best. Inattention is plain bad manners.

2. *Be Objective*. This is a quality of many aspects. The objective person searches for truth, that is, for authoritative, usable fact. He judges well how much he knows, how much more he needs to know, before he can reach a sound, dependable conclusion. He is receptive to the data and the thought of others. He is not dogmatic or argumentative. His demeanor is thoughtful, his mode of expression is pitched in a low key. He neither vocalizes nor gesticulates aggressively. He tends to use expressions like "I am much interested in what you say" or "I think Mr. Doe has a strong point" or "I would like to hear more on this matter" or "I may be wrong but it does seem to me that."

The objective person knows how hard it is to be objective and so comes close to being so.

3. *Be Informed*. One objective of discussion is to inform. Obviously, the more you know the more you help to carry out the objective. Being informed means much more than having opinions and vague information. It means that you have studied the question, you have gathered,

documented, and filed material (see section on page 12, "You Do Research"). One trouble with many discussions is that the members of a group tend to depend too much on others for information. The result is, no one really knows anything. In this case, discussion is pooled ignorance.

4. *Talk enough, neither too much nor too little.* Be neither a monopolist nor the strong, silent type. If wisdom at times is identified with taciturnity, it is more often discernible in those who talk. Again, however, it is not often discernible in those who talk too much.

Many of us have had the experience of being so unsure of ourselves that we do not say something that comes to our minds. If this happens once, it easily happens again, and then again; our shyness turns to embarrassment, our inhibition to muteness. The idea of speaking at all makes our hearts pound and our hands perspire. We feel upon us the eyes of the pitying; our sense of inadequacy deepens. The cure? Say whatever comes to you. Do not worry the idea with this way of saying it or that; just say it, and if they don't like it, so what? You have at least expressed yourself. And yours may be the view that prevails.

5. *Be easy to listen to.* To begin with, you should be easily heard. You do not mumble; you do not go along in dead level monotony. The quiet manner can be unintelligible. It can also be dull. But don't be too loud or too emphatic either. Discussion is not the place for aggressive debating. It is not a place for persuasive oratory.

But you may speak with emphasis. While persuasion is not the aim of discussion, this does not mean that you may not express yourself with earnestness and zest. Do not a mollycoddle be, nor yet a vacillator, the breed that hems and haws around on any question. If you have a conviction, then express it clearly—and emphatically.

6. *Stick to the point.* If the point under discussion in regard to improving education is teachers' salaries, don't jump to the lack of physics and mathematics courses in many high schools. One point at a time is the rule. A fertile cause of confusion and irritation in group thinking is the inability of chairman and participants to finish with one question before they go to another. Don't be afraid, if the chairman is lax, to ask a member who is straying far and wide to come back to the point. I assume that you would ask with tact.

7. *Watch your language.* Beware of words that muddle thought and trigger emotional reactions, words that confuse, embarrass, wound, and anger (see earlier section on page 34, "Words That Hinder Clear Think-

ing"). Avoid the words we called *fuzzy, highfalutin, fighting, scary, souped-up,* and *tricky.* They distort and mislead, they frighten and embitter, they foment intellectual and emotional disorder, even lead to fisticuffs and gunfire.

Strive only for accuracy and clarity.

THE DISCUSSION LEADER

1. *He stays in the background.* He is not a busybody. He is not forever inserting his own opinions. He does not find it necessary to restate —"more clearly"—everything that is said. He restates only when clarity is missing or when something deserves emphasis. There are chairmen who take themselves too seriously, who see themselves as God's gift to lesser folk, and the result is endless meddling.

2. *He stimulates.* True, he stays in the background as a rule, but what if the participants stay there too? The chairman needs then to come to the fore. He may ask challenging questions, he may point out issues that have not been touched, he may indicate shortages of evidence, he may even disagree, provocatively, with what someone has said. To stay in the background does not mean to become a nonentity. The chairman is above all a leader; he sometimes has to be provocative to discharge his function.

3. *He keeps the peace.* If a question is a hot one, discussion can turn into debate, which then turns into clamorous charge and countercharge and name-calling. The chairman must now be a Solomon. He must wisely mediate among the adversaries and salve their wounds. Specifically, he may do the following:

(a) As Abraham Lincoln could do when the going was rough and feeling ran high, he could tell a pertinent joke.

(b) He seems to ignore the fracas. He might say something like this: "We have just shown how interested we all are in this matter. We have a hard problem to solve and we're doing quite well. May I suggest one or two important things to get to before we adjourn."

(c) He may have to be severe. He might say, "John, you've said enough. You too, Joe, and you, Jim, and you Miss Potts. We've had it. Now I want each of you to cool off before you say another word. Meanwhile, the others of us will talk a bit."

(d) If all else fails, he simply says, "The meeting is adjourned."

4. *He guides the discussion.* He has a tentative pattern to follow. His topical outline, which the participants may have a copy of, is flexible

but it will in all probability be followed. Yet he should avoid imposing it. If a member wanders from a point under discussion, he should be brought back, but not prematurely. Often a member seems to be off the topic but then he shows that he isn't or he comes back of his own accord.

Sometimes the chairman summarizes: when a certain phase of the question has been covered, when a good deal of data has been introduced and there is danger of losing track of the specific issue involved, and when the discussion ends.

5. *He is a reflective thinker.* He knows what makes for valid data and sound reasoning. He may advise the participants that too little data have been brought forth on a matter and that therefore it would be risky to come to a decision. He may point out weaknesses in statistics, in testimony or source, in reasoning. But he must be not too ready to do all this; let the participants have a chance, a good chance, to do the critical thinking.

6. *He is the soul of tact.* He can be gentle but firm, genial but tough, patient but decisive. He has a sense of humor, which, however, he does not exploit too much. His fairness is a steady light for all to see. He is neither demanding not domineering; he is slow to anger and never descends to the tactics of the cockpit. Tact is the gentle art of a thorough democrat; it is abiding, sensitive respect for others. If a chairman has intelligence and tact, what more could we want?

Other Specific Duties of the Chairman

1. He introduces the participants to each other and to the audience. He seats them in a face to face formation, except for the symposium, where they face the audience.

2. He provides water and glasses, if needed. He looks after the ventilation. He takes care of coats and hats if necessary.

3. If a speaker's stand is desired, he arranges for it. If a public address system is used, he has it tested for working order.

4. He moderates the audience participation session. He explains how the session is to be conducted:

(a) Questions may be written and brought up to the chairman or they may be asked from the floor.

(b) One question at a time. No person may get by with "I have three questions to ask. . . ."

(c) Not more than two minutes for a question or a comment. Make it clear that the rule will be enforced. In cases where you anticipate a real problem in limiting speeches, have a timekeeper who has a "loud alarum bell."

5. If a member of the audience goes off on a tangent, the chairman brings him back.

6. If a member abuses another, the chairman checks him.

7. If one member talks and five minutes later wants to talk again when someone who has not talked wishes to be heard, the chairman recognizes the latter.

11 PARLIAMENTARY PROCEDURE

AN ORGANIZATION OR ACTION GROUP THAT MEETS REGU-
larly usually follows parliamentary procedure. But sometimes a method
is used called consensus. This method is based on the premise that well-
intentioned people if given enough time to discuss a problem will come
through with a wise decision. The trouble with the method is that it
overdoes "group think," it overdoes group priority. Parliamentary procedure may allow the maverick or the ornery minority too much recognition, but consensus homogenizes. Consensus is fine for like-minded
people but who is to make the Jovian judgment that any group of people
is like-minded?

Parliamentary procedure not only protects the rights of the minority;
it also—and this we tend to forget—protects the rights of the majority.
If properly handled, it keeps the minority, no matter how fervent, under
control. It keeps the minority from recklessly obstructing the wishes of
the majority.

Parliamentary procedure expedites the transaction of business. Yet if
delay is necessary, this is made possible; if reconsideration is desired,
this is possible. Parliamentary procedure offers human beings ample
opportunity to correct their mistakes, enlarge their understanding, and
clarify their actions.

The seasoned user of parliamentary procedure knows when to dispense with the letter of the law. It is only the immature dabbler who is
always coming up with piddling objections, who insists on dotting all
the i's and crossing all the t's. Admittedly the temptation is strong for
novices in the business to make a great show of their new-found knowledge, but this is usually a passing stage and it does have its credit side:
only by indulging in the complexities of procedure do you emerge with
an appreciation of the beauties of simplicity, in this branch of human
endeavor as in so many other branches.

Our concern here is only with the principles and means of parliamentary procedure in common use. We avoid detailed listings of tech-
nicalities and exceptions.

THE AGENDA OF A MEETING

1. You take the roll.

2. You call the meeting to order.

3. The minutes of the last meeting are read, and corrected if necessary. No motion is needed to approve the minutes; the chairman says, "Any corrections of the minutes?" He pauses a decent interval and then says, "If there are none, the minutes are approved." Or he says if there were corrections, "Any further corrections?" Again he pauses, then he says, "If not, the minutes are approved." The only time a motion is needed to approve the minutes is when there is disagreement about their accuracy and about proposed corrections.

The minutes may be detailed or brief, depending on what the group prefers. A record of the motions made and the disposition of them is all that is needed. But the group may also want recorded the names of everyone who spoke and what they said, even to the point of a verbatim account.

4. Notices are read.

5. Reports of standing and special committees are read. The reading of the reports means that they are *received;* a motion to *receive* is not needed and is out of order. A motion to *adopt* or *accept* is needed if action is to be considered.

6. Unfinished business. There may be postponed matters to consider. Again, the previous meeting may have had to adjourn before action could be taken.

7. New business. This means new matters not yet considered.

8. The meeting is adjourned.

YOUR DISCUSSION RIGHTS

1. You are entitled to speak twice on the same question the same day and ten minutes each time. But if an amendment to a motion is moved, the question is considered different and you may speak twice on it. The same applies to any other debatable motion that might be made. If you wish to speak more than twice on a particular question, the assembly by a two-thirds vote can permit you to do so.

2. You are entitled to recognition by the chair if you are the first to request it unless you have already spoken and others wish to speak, or unless the maker of the motion who has not spoken wishes to speak.

3. When you speak, do not make slighting remarks about any mem-

bers. This is ground for a point of personal privilege by an aggrieved member and can lead to your censure.

4. You may interrupt a speaker to ask a question; he need not answer it. If he does answer it, the time taken comes out of his regular allotment. Remember this if someone interrupts you. The form to follow in interrupting to ask a question is: "Mr. Chairman, I should like to ask the speaker a question." The chair then asks the speaker if he is willing to answer.

YOUR VOTING RIGHTS

1. You may vote by voice—"All those in favor say, 'Aye'; all opposed say, 'No'." You may vote by show of hands or by rising, by roll call or by secret ballot. To vote by roll call or ballot unless it is required in the by-laws of an organization must be authorized by a majority vote. Roll call means that you call out the name of each member, who then answers "Yes" or "No," "Yea" or "Nay."

2. If in the case of a close voice or hand vote you are not satisfied that the chair has announced the correct result, you may say, "I call for a division of the assembly." If your call is seconded, the chair is obligated to take a standing vote.

3. Remember, the chair can vote to make or break a tie.

4. If you have an intimate personal interest in the outcome, you should abstain from voting. This is so much a matter of individual conscience and sense of propriety that it is difficult to generalize. You may, however, with complete immunity to public attitude, vote for yourself for an office. If you want the office, you would be foolish not to vote for yourself.

5. You may change your vote at any time before the chair announces the outcome.

6. Not every matter need be put to a regular vote. If the chair believes that there is virtual unanimity on a matter, he may invoke the principle of general consent, like this: "If there are no objections, we shall consider the motion passed." But if someone objects, then the regular procedure must be followed. The seasoned chairman may use this device often, without irritating the members.

7. Remember, a majority vote means a majority of the members actually voting, blanks or abstentions not counted. A two-thirds vote means two-thirds of the members actually voting, blanks and abstentions not

counted. A two-thirds vote of the entire membership may at times be stipulated in the by-laws.

THE MOST COMMON MOTIONS*

1. *The Main Motion.* This is the motion that initiates business. Without a main motion, obviously no action of any kind can be taken.

You make this motion in one of three ways:

"I move that the dues be raised."

"I make a motion that the dues be raised."

"Be it resolved that the dues be raised."

2. *To postpone indefinitely.* This motion is designed to kill a main motion. It also offers opponents of a main motion a chance for a test vote. If the motion to postpone indefinitely is not passed, the opponents of the main motion still have another chance to vote it down.

3. *To amend.* You may move to amend certain motions and you may move to amend an amendment.

Suppose a main motion were: "I move that the dues be raised." You can amend by adding, by striking out, by striking out and inserting. Someone moves to amend by adding at the end of the motion the words "Fifty cents." If this is seconded, it and it alone becomes the immediately pending question. Now someone moves to amend the amendment by adding "Payable twice a year." If seconded, it and it alone becomes the immediately pending question. Suppose the amendment to the amendment is passed. The pending question becomes the amendment as amended, to wit: "Fifty cents, payable twice a year." If this is passed, the question becomes the main motion as amended: "The dues be raised fifty cents, payable twice a year."

The trouble with many efforts to amend is that the proposed amendment is not exactly stated, nor is the part at which the amendment is aimed made precise. In the simple sentence above, there is no problem. But what if the main motion were complicated, having many parts, as a bill before Congress. Novices in parliamentary procedure often get all mixed up in the amendment process. Be sure that you state exactly what your amendment is and where it fits.

The so-called substitute motion aims to amend by striking out a whole motion. If passed, it is not adopted, it only becomes the immediately pending question.

* See table, p. 138.

An amendment is out of order that merely proposes the negative of a positive statement, like inserting "not" before "raised" in the question, "the dues be raised."

4. *To refer to a committee.* This happens when a group wants intensive investigation of a matter. The committee may be special, standing, or a committee of the whole which means that the whole group becomes a committee—"I move that this assembly become a committee of the whole." This enables a group to discuss informally a question, without being hedged in by the regulations of formal procedure.

But a matter is usually referred to a standing or a special committee. A common weakness in the motion to commit is a failure to stipulate what standing committee and if a special committee how it should be selected. If you want a special committee of three members to be appointed by the chair, say so in your motion. If you want it to be a committee of five members elected by the assembly, say so: "Mr. Chairman, I move that the question of raising the dues be referred to a special committee of five members to be elected by this group and that the committee report its recommendations at our next regular meeting." Note in this motion that *what* and *when* the committee should report are also stipulated. In short, you should make a motion to commit complete and specific.

5. *To postpone to a definite time.* This gives further time for consideration and also insures consideration.

In making this motion you might say:

"I move that the question of raising the dues be postponed to our next regular meeting to be considered right after the minutes are approved."

or

"I move that the question be postponed to 10:15 A.M. at our next regular meeting."

6. *To change the limits of debate.* This motion can do many things: (1) limit the total time of debate, (2) limit the total number of speeches, (3) limit the members to one speech each, (4) extend the speaking time of a member or members, (5) increase the number of speeches of a member or members. Because it aims at one of the fundamental rights of a democratic society, freedom of speech with due regard for others, it requires for passage a two-thirds vote.

7. *Previous questions.* This motion cuts off debate and requires,

therefore, a two-thirds vote to pass. It aims to bring a debatable question to an immediate vote. The motion is made as follows: "Mr. Chairman, I move the previous question."

The motion is often misunderstood. To vote on it is not to vote on the question to which it applies. The only effect of a vote on it is to stop or not to stop debate on the question to which it applies.

8. *To lay on the table.* This motion is often misused as a device to kill a question. The only purpose of it is to delay or postpone action. If you wish to kill a question, try either the motion to postpone indefinitely or the one, discussed below, to object to consideration. Either of these is proper, the first because it is debatable, the second because, since it is not debatable, it requires a two-thirds vote. The motion to lay on the table is not debatable and still requires only a majority vote. Therefore, to use the motion to kill a question strikes a blow at freedom of discussion. You can only interfere with this freedom if you have ample opportunity to debate a proposal to curb it or if a two-thirds vote is required to pass the proposal.

9. *To take from the table.* This motion returns to consideration a question that was laid on the table. It is not in order immediately after a question has been laid on the table. It may be made only after other business has intervened.

10. *To withdraw a motion.* The maker of a motion may withdraw it upon his request alone up to the time the chair puts it to the assembly for discussion. After it has been put, or stated, by the chair, it can only be withdrawn if the assembly does not object. If even one person objects, the matter is put to a vote; a majority is required to allow withdrawal. The consent of the seconder is never required. If instead of asking to withdraw the motion, you ask to change it, the seconder may withdraw his second, in which case someone else would have to second the motion.

11. *To suspend a rule.* This requires a two-thirds vote to pass, for the reason that you are overturning established practice with all the evils that such action might entail. But you cannot vote to suspend, even with a unanimous vote, clauses or by-laws of a constitution. You can only vote to suspend rules of parliamentary procedure.

12. *To object to consideration.* A two-thirds vote is required for this undebatable motion since it aims to prevent the consideration of a question.

13. *To appeal from the decision of the chair.* Any ruling of the chair

may be appealed by any member. You would say: "Mr. Chairman, I appeal from the decision of the chair." The chairman should then say: "Shall the decision of the chair be sustained?" Debate is in order only if the ruling is made while a debatable question is immediately pending. Thus the appeal may be discussed if a ruling is made when a motion to refer to a committee is immediately pending; an appeal may not be discussed if the ruling is made while a motion to object to consideration is immediately pending. But in any case the chair has the right to state his reasons for the ruling.

A majority vote is required to reject a motion to sustain the decision of the chair. If the vote is a tie, the chair is sustained. The chair may vote to make the vote a tie.

Obstructionists can easily abuse the privilege of appeal. The chair should not be shy about calling such elements out of order.

14. *Point of order.* A point of order may be made if an irregularity in procedure seems to have occurred. You would say: "Mr. Chairman, point of order," or "I rise to a point of order." The chair would say: "State your point of order." After you state it, he will say: "Your point of order is accepted" or "rejected." If you are not satisfied with the ruling, you may appeal from the decision of the chair.

The point of order should be distinguished from the point of personal privilege which applies not to rules of procedure but to the privileges of a person as a member of the assembly. You may make a point of personal privilege if your motives have been questioned by a member or if you feel your speaking privileges have been flouted.

The point of privilege may be raised in behalf of the assembly. Perhaps a vacant office has not been filled or the minutes have not been properly kept. Or maybe the ventilation of the room is bad or there is noise or there are not enough seats.

But there are people who seem to get delicious pleasure out of points of order and points of privilege. Or else they are supersensitive. How else explain their alacrity in making the points?

15. *To reconsider and to rescind.* These two motions should be considered together because they are often confused. The motion to reconsider, if passed, simply annuls the vote on a question and brings the question up for a second consideration; a vote to rescind repeals the action—it is as if no action were ever taken. The motion to reconsider can only be made by persons who voted with the prevailing side and can be made only on the day or the day after an action was voted, holidays

and Saturdays and Sundays not counted. The motion to rescind can be made only if the motion to reconsider cannot be made. In other words, someone who did not vote with the prevailing side may move to rescind an action on the same day it was taken or the day following but he may not move to reconsider on those days. Conversely a person who can *legitimately* make a motion to reconsider cannot make one to rescind.

The motion to reconsider requires a majority vote. The motion to rescind requires, if no previous notice has been given of intention to make the motion, a two-thirds vote; if notice has been given, a majority vote.

Neither of the motions is in order if irrevocable steps have been taken to put into effect action that was taken.

16. *Special order.* This motion not only postpones a question to a certain time but it compells consideration at that time even though another question is then under discussion. A simple motion to postpone to a certain time allows a pending question to be disposed of before the postponed question comes up. Since a special order has such preemptive power, it needs a two-thirds vote to pass. You would make the motion as follows: "Mr. Chairman, I move that the question of raising the dues be postponed to our next regular meeting, at 10:30 A.M., and that it be made a special order."

17. *To adjourn.* The motion to adjourn has high privilege or priority. Only one motion (see the table of motions) has higher rank, the motion to fix the time for the next meeting. It would be too bad to adjourn before a next meeting could be set if such a meeting had to be set.

Since the motion to adjourn has such high priority, it must not be abused, the more so because it requires only a majority vote to pass. The motion should not be made to prevent consideration of a question. It should not be made as soon as a special meeting has been called to order; a special meeting has a definite, urgent purpose and time must be allowed to consider the matter. While the motion to adjourn may be made repeatedly at a meeting, it should not be made again until substantial discussion or other business has intervened.

18. *To fix the time for the next meeting.* If an organization does not meet regularly, it is of the highest urgency that a meeting is not adjourned until the time for the next meeting has been fixed. No motion takes priority over this one.

The table below shows the parliamentary ranks, and other characteristics, of motions. Rank pertains to the technical priority of motions.

While the main motion introduces basic business and while other motions would be pointless without it, it is still the lowest motion in rank.

To illustrate how rank would work, suppose someone moved to raise the dues fifty cents. The motion was seconded. Then someone moved to amend by striking out *fifty* and inserting *seventy-five*. This was seconded. The proposed amendment is now the immediately pending question: it and it alone is up for discussion. Now someone moves to refer the question to a committee of five appointed by the chair. The motion is seconded. It becomes the immediately pending question: it and it alone is debatable. Then Mr. X moves to lay the question on the table. Someone seconds. This motion is not debatable. But before a vote can be taken, Mr. Y moves to postpone the question to the next regular meeting at 11:30 A.M. and that it be made a *special order*. Note the high rank of this motion. If seconded, it supercedes the motion to lay on the table as the immediately pending question. If it is defeated, then the motion to lay on the table takes over again. We hope that a matter would not reach this degree of complication, but if it did, the table below would be a sure guide.

So the rank of motions means (1) when a motion of higher rank than another is made, it becomes the question that has to be considered; (2) when a motion of a certain rank is under consideration, no motion of a lower rank can be made.

Take the Table of Motions with you to meetings. Do not be upset over your inability at first to remember the details of motions. Work with the table, practice it, and you will come to use it as well as anyone else.

You will note that there are five incidental motions, all having the same rank. Priority among them depends on which motion is made first. If any one of them is immediately pending, no other one of them can be made.

NOMINATION PROCEDURES

If the procedure in making nominations is not specified in the by-laws of an organization or is not standardized by regular practice, then a motion to stipulate procedure is necessary. The motion may provide that nominations be made from the chairman or by ballot or by mail. It is open to amendment.

If nominations have been made by a committee, it is still in order to make nominations from the floor. Nominations do not require a second, though in practice several members may second a particular nomination, as at a political convention. A motion to close nominations is technically in order at any time but it should not be used until the assembly has had plenty of time to make nominations. Since it tends to restrict the right of members to select their representatives, it requires a two-thirds vote to pass. A motion to reopen nominations may also be made; this requires only a majority vote.

The best way to vote for nominees is by ballot. Any other way tends to pressure certain voters.

THE CHAIRMAN OF A MEETING

Whatever I said earlier about the qualifications and duties of a discussion leader applies to a chairman of a meeting. But because he now possess powers arising from his presumed knowledge of parliamentary law, and because the members of the group look to him for procedural efficiency, I stress certain qualities he ought to have.

He should be decisive, yet not too decisive lest he be considered a dictator. He should be fair, but be careful not to lean over backward to favor troublesome members or a fervent minority. He must take pains to let everybody and every faction have their say. The hotter an issue is, the more he is on the spot to guarantee a fair hearing for all.

If you, as chairman, take part in a heated discussion, watch out: you will be damned by many. You should be careful not to use your office to give you special advantage. If you do feel impelled to express an opinion, have regard for the amenities in some such way, as follows:

"If I may, I should like to make a few remarks"

or

"I know I may be off base in speaking at this time, but I hope you will not mind too much if I say what I feel I have to say"

or

"Well, such is my opinion. Thank you for hearing me out."

Not that you should be hypocritical, rather that you should be diplomatic. Be neither abject nor bumptious. Be a leader who is neither servile nor overbearing.

If you have to call a member out of order, do so in the knowledge that few relish being called out of order. If you have to rule a motion dilatory or frivolous, keep in mind that those supporting the motion do not see it that way. Know the law but do not parade your knowledge. You may suggest to members ways to expedite or postpone business but only when it is necessary or when the members ask help. Know when to dispense with the letter of the law, as when you make use of the technique of general consent—"Any objections? If not, the motion is passed."

In the interests of clarity and efficiency, the chairman should be sure to do the following:

1. Before discussion begins, state exactly the motion as made.

2. Before putting a question to a vote, state it exactly.

3. Before putting a question to a vote, ask, if necessary, whether it is clear to everybody.

4. After the vote, state the result and, if necessary, the practical effect of the action: "The motion to refer the question of raising the dues to a special committee of five to be appointed by the chair has been passed. I will in the next day or two announce the committee and I ask that the committee report to us at our next regular meeting. The committee, from the wording of the motion that was passed, may confine itself to gathering information but there is nothing to stop it from also making recommendations."

TABLE OF MOTIONS

Motion	Need of Second	Can be Amended
A. PRIVILEGED MOTIONS		
1. To fix time for next meeting	Yes	Yes
2. To adjourn	Yes	No
3. Question of privilege	No	No
4. Special order	No	No
B. SPECIAL MOTIONS		
5. To reconsider	Yes	No
6. To rescind	Yes	Yes
C. INCIDENTAL MOTIONS		
7. Point of order	No	No
7. To appeal from chair	Yes	No
7. To object to consideration	No	No
7. To suspend a rule	Yes	No
7. To withdraw a motion	No	No
D. SUBSIDIARY MOTIONS		
8. To take from the table	Yes	No
9. To lay on table	Yes	No
10. Previous question	Yes	No
11. To limit or extend the limit of debate	Yes	Yes
12. To postpone to a definite time	Yes	Yes
13. To commit, refer, recommit	Yes	Yes
14. To amend	Yes	Yes
15. To postpone indefinitely	Yes	No
E. PRINCIPAL MOTIONS		
16. Any main question	Yes	Yes

Debatable	Vote Required	May Be Re-considered	May Be Laid on Table
No (usually)	Majority	No	No
No	Majority	No	No
No	Chairman (may be appealed)	No	No
No	Two-thirds	No	No
Yes	Majority	No	Yes
Yes	Two-thirds, no notice; majority with notice	Aff. vote— no	Yes
No	Chairman (may be appealed)	No	No
Yes	Majority	Yes	No
No	Two-thirds	Aff. vote— no	No
No	Two-thirds	No	No
No	Majority	Yes	Yes
No	Majority	No	No
No	Majority	No	No
No	Two-thirds	If lost, no	Yes
No	Two-thirds	No	No
Yes	Majority	Yes	Yes
Yes	Majority	Yes	Yes
Yes	Majority	Yes	Yes
Yes	Majority	Yes	Yes
Yes	Majority	Yes	Yes

INDEX

ORVIN LARSON, Professor and Chairman of the Department of Speech and Theatre at Brooklyn College, was born in Minneapolis, Minnesota, raised in Sioux Falls, South Dakota, and educated at Augustana College in Sioux Falls, and the State University of Iowa. A lecturer and writer of wide experience in the field of speech including television and stage, he has taught also at the Universities of Denver, Hawaii, and Indiana.